All About
INVESTING IN GOLD

OTHER TITLES IN THE "ALL ABOUT" FINANCE SERIES

All About
INVESTING
IN GOLD

THE EASY WAY TO GET STARTED

JOHN JAGERSON
S. WADE HANSEN

New York   Chicago   San Francisco   Lisbon   London   Madrid
Mexico City   Milan   New Delhi   San Juan   Seoul
Singapore   Sydney   Toronto

The *McGraw·Hill* Companies

1 2 3 4 5 6 7 8 9 10   DOC/DOC   1 5 4 3 2 1

ISBN: 978-0-07-176834-4
MHID: 0-07-176834-3

e-ISBN: 978-0-07-176835-1
e-MHID: 0-07-176835-1

This publication is designed to provide accurate and authoritative information in regard to the subject matter covered. It is sold with the understanding that neither the author nor the publisher is engaged in rendering legal, accounting, securities trading, or other professional services. If legal advice or other expert assistance is required, the services of a competent professional person should be sought.
—*From a Declaration of Principles Jointly Adopted by*
a Committee of the American Bar Association and
a Committee of Publishers and Associations

Library of Congress Cataloging-in-Publication Data
Jagerson, John.
  All about investing in gold / by John Jagerson and S. Wade Hansen.
    p. cm.
  ISBN 978-0-07-176834-4 (alk. paper)
  1. Gold.   2. Investments.   I. Hansen, S. Wade.   II. Title.
  HG293.J34 2011
  332.63—dc22

                                                                011008762

McGraw-Hill books are available at special quantity discounts to use as premiums and sales promotions or for use in corporate training programs. To contact a representative, please e-mail us at bulksales@mcgraw-hill.com.

This book is printed on acid-free paper.

This book is dedicated to Wendi, Heather, and Lance—thanks for all your help. We would also like to thank Morgan Ertel and the production team at McGraw-Hill for giving us the opportunity and such excellent support. Finally, thanks to A.A. and B.F.B for being so steadfast and firm in your encouragement.

—*John Jagerson*

To my fabulous wife and three wonderful boys.

—*S. Wade Hansen*

Contents

Chapter 4

Chapter 5

Chapter 6

Chapter 7

Chapter 8

Chapter 9

All About
INVESTING
IN GOLD

INTRODUCTION

Gold trading and investing has become much easier and cheaper, and that is good news for long-term investors and short-term traders who are looking for more opportunities and diversification. It has been the best performing major asset class over the last five years, returning more than 200 percent on an unleveraged basis, and that trend seems likely to continue for the next five years.[1] Gold traders have unprecedented access to investment products that are both cheap and efficient. It is now possible to invest in gold bullion for fees as low as 0.25 percent per year. Many of these products are new innovations; that is not a bad thing, but it does require caution and education before one makes an investment.

The introduction and growing popularity of gold exchange-traded funds (ETFs), fractional gold futures contracts, and legitimate bullion storage services are quickly displacing the outrageously expensive and unstable products that traditionally dominated the gold market. Demand for gold as an investment is growing within markets as diverse as the United States, where investors are seeking protection from financial market disruptions, and China, where gold

---

[1] iShares Gold Trust (IAU).

1

investors are buying record amounts as a way to hedge against out-of-control inflation. Chinese investors demanded 45.1 tonnes (metric tons) of gold in the third quarter of 2010, a new quarterly record.[2] Chinese buying accounted for 16 percent of total global demand for gold in that quarter. We can only imagine what will happen when the world's biggest saver decides to really get serious about gold investing.

During the five-year period 2005–2010 large-cap stocks returned less than 5 percent, riskier small-cap stocks returned less than 25 percent, and even the surprising bull market for Treasury bond funds provided only 10 percent for investors with nearly perfect timing. Don't misunderstand those numbers: They are not annual returns. These are total returns for all five years combined. As an investor, you are probably well aware of the poor performance of many assets over the last 5, 10, or even 15 years and agree that something has gone very wrong with the traditional investment choices. Smart traders are making a decision to use gold as a way to limit account volatility and improve performance.

Stock investors have been hurt by volatile markets. The Standard & Poor's 500 (S&P 500) closed 2010 with a net loss of 10 percent for the decade, whereas over the same period gold was up more than 400 percent. If you have been investing exclusively in stocks, we have a lot to show you about adding gold to your portfolio and how it can be done without adding any complexity or disrupting your brokerage account. You still need to be careful not to become a *return chaser* in the rush to profits in the gold market. We will show you how to balance your new gold holdings to provide the maximum benefits without taking on too much risk.

We think the fundamentals in the market are pointing to a long-term and substantial increase in the price of gold. In this book we will present the reasons for our bullish bias and specific actions we recommend for taking advantage of gold as an investment.

---

[2] World Gold Council, "Gold Demand Trends Q3 2010."

However, we are also realists and know that the market is full of *fat tail risks* that are impossible to predict and can shift market fundamentals without warning. Gold investors should be prepared for changes, and we will show you how to profit even if prices do not rise as expected. "Markets can remain irrational a lot longer than you and I can remain solvent," wrote the economist John Maynard Keynes, and we agree with that sentiment. There is no reason to feel trapped in old or erroneous analysis when you can be making money instead.

ABOUT US

We are two of the founders and analysts at LearningMarkets.com. We launched the site because we feel that within the world of financial content there is a significant gap in education that is actionable enough to be useful but honest enough not to be dangerous. We plan to continue providing that kind of content for new gold traders in this book.

We have been working with individual investors in the gold, forex, stocks, and options markets for several years, and after talking to thousands of investors, we have been surprised by how easy it is to avoid the most common trading mistakes but how seldom investors are aware that they are sabotaging their performance. These problems tend to get worse when a particular market, such as gold, is very hot. The questions we get about gold from readers today are no different from the questions we got about stocks in 1999 or real estate in 2006, and the answers are also the same. Consistent traders who avoid the hype and use a disciplined approach to the market with a focus on reducing costs and account volatility will be the most successful. Promoting that kind of approach to the gold market is our mission, and we are very passionate about achieving our objectives.

We also can speak from personal experience as individual and professional investors. We know what it feels like to make trading decisions that are emotionally challenging. We have worked on the brokerage side of the business as well as being professional advisors, and we can tell you that there are plenty of traders who are investing very successfully in the gold market. The skills those traders used to make profits in the market are not a secret, and we can show you what they do and why they do it.

HOW TO READ THIS BOOK

Knowing your audience is necessary if you are going to write a book that will be useful to your readers. We have an advantage in this respect because we talk to our readers on a daily basis at our site, www.LearningMarkets.com. One of the things we know about our audience members is that some have a lot more experience than others but they all tend to share most of the same long-term objectives. We wrote this book with those facts in mind and included the necessary background information to support new investors but also included enough detail to make it useful to experienced traders who are interested in getting into the gold market with new strategies. This book should be a reference as you make investing decisions and does not need to be read front to back if you do not need the same background a new trader might require.

For example, if you are already an active options or ETF trader, that's great because we are too. You might want to start with a few of the option strategies we recommend for long- and short-term traders and then go back to the products section to learn more about why we suggest certain gold ETF and stock options over the alternatives. If you are new to investing but are willing to put in some work, that's even better. We suggest that you start from the beginning and take it one step at a time. Practice will help you learn to apply the material, and we have several suggestions about the tools and support you will need to get some risk-free experience. Either way we are excited to engage with you on a daily basis and continue the discussion at www.LearningMarkets.com, where we provide daily live (all free) videos and commentary covering the gold, stocks, and forex markets.

WHAT YOU WILL LEARN FROM THE BOOK

Gold is a hot topic right now, so it isn't a surprise to see an increase in the flow of books, videos, and other educational products that promise to help you become successful in the market. We have been buying and reading books about the gold market for a long time, and there are a few that are excellent, but most . . . not so much. The worst gold books and education products tend to fit one of two templates. They are either 300-page diatribes on the evils of monetarists, central banking, fiscal deficit spending, and global conspiracies or they offer some vague strategies you can use to get rich quick by becoming an active gold trader or bullion investor.

Though the doomsday prophets may turn out to be right in saying that central banking and fiat currencies will be the downfall of Western civilization, the information they provide is not really that practical. What we intend to do is bridge the gap and provide a starting place for professional and individual investors interested in getting involved in the gold market. There is more than one way to acquire gold exposure, and some methods are better than others, depending on one's individual objectives. We will dig into the nuanced differences between products and strategies to help you build a plan and a gold product mix that fit you as an investor.

We tend to consider ourselves investing skeptics, which means that the more confident an analyst is about her forecast, the more dubious we become. We are equally skeptical of Federal Reserve board members, Internet-based gold bullion sales groups, and fund managers. In our experience the more confident an analyst is about where he thinks the market (gold or otherwise) is going, the more likely it is that he is pitching a product of some kind. It doesn't matter if that "product" is mail-order gold bullion or political support for another round of quantitative easing; being skeptical will help you survive. This means that although we have a bullish bias toward gold prices in the long term, we also know that forecast could be wrong. There are analysts in the market we call broken clocks because they say the same thing year after year, and like a broken clock, if we wait long enough, they may turn out to be right. But can you withstand market volatility in the meantime?

Gold bulls in the 1980s and 1990s dealt with a flat market for two decades. It is unlikely that we could have remained confidently bullish for that long in the face of an underwhelming trend if gold had been our only investment. History often repeats itself, and that kind of situation could happen again. Even more disconcerting is the thought that it is possible for gold to enter a long-term bear market. If you aren't prepared for those times when your analysis turns out to be wrong, you could become trapped in two decades worth of losses and opportunity costs. Figure I-1 shows the long flat trend in gold that lasted for 25 years. Although patience eventually was

FIGURE I-1

Spot gold prices, January 1980–December 2005.

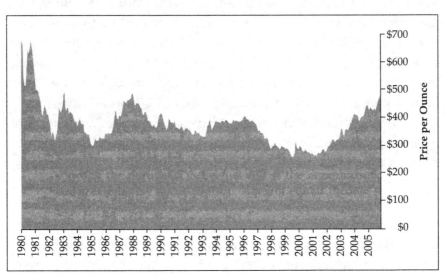

Source: World Gold Council

rewarded, many small traders left the market to avoid what seemed like endless value erosion.

We think one reason so many authors and analysts take such a hard line about gold prices going up endlessly is that they are pushing products that are very difficult to modify. For example, if you buy bullion, as many analysts recommend, gold prices must continue to rise for that investment to be profitable because buying and selling gold coins or bullion is difficult and expensive. Holding a hard commodity like that is the ultimate in bullish bets, and it is usually much more lucrative for the bullion dealer than it is for the investor. In the spirit of full disclosure, you should know that unlike many authors, we do not have any gold products to sell you, but we do have positions in gold from time to time in our own accounts. We hope to use that to our advantage in this book by inserting as much real-market experience as possible.

We intend to spend very little time proving that our bullish forecast is correct. We will make that argument as a way to help you understand the fundamentals of the gold market, but the most valuable subject covered will be how to understand future changes in the gold market and the strategies to profit from those changes. If gold continues to rise and reaches $4,000 an ounce, we will be very happy, but if prices do not do that, we will show you how to be proactive and profit from the unexpected. This is good news for new gold investors because unlike the stock market, a bear market or flat trend in gold is not a bad thing. Gold prices often fall when the global economy is doing well, and depending on your strategy, trading a flat gold market with exchange-listed products such as ETFs, futures, and options could be even safer, less expensive, and more profitable than just buying and holding bullion.

These background comments are important to establish the context for the rest of the book. Some of our opinions about the gold market and gold products are controversial, but they have roots in real-life experience. The nature of the market is to periodically do the thing we expect the least. If that were not true, there wouldn't be any profits available to investors willing to take risks. This is good news because a trader who can make changes will be able to walk away a winner regardless of what the market does. We wrote this book to be just as valuable 5 or 10 years from now, when gold is entering a new bear market, as it is right now while gold is hot.

How to Set Realistic Expectations

As we communicate with the investing community, we get to talk to very successful (and happy) traders, but as you can imagine, we also talk to many more traders who are frustrated, stressed, and unsuccessful. A common denominator among the latter group is unrealistic expectations. We can't show you how to get rich quick by investing in gold—no one can. We can't show you how to make 100 percent per year or 5 percent per month in the gold market either, and we definitely can't show you why gold is the best investment class and is guaranteed to outpace all other investments for the next 20 years.

In fact, if you have heard any of those promises from other sources, books, seminars, or Internet ads, do yourself a favor and head in the other direction. It's not realistic because the future is too uncertain. That is the underlying premise of risk taking. If uncertainty didn't exist, there would be no opportunity for profit because there would be no need for risk takers and speculators in the first place. An unavoidable law of the financial markets is that risk and reward are positively correlated. That means that if you want to have the potential for big gains, you need to take similarly big risks.

There is a similar trade-off between effort and return. There are some very easy ways to invest in the gold market that require little effort and maintenance, but the more disconnected you are from your investing, the lower the potential return is. This isn't a problem, it's a reality, and the trade-off of less effort and stress for more time and flexibility may be a good thing, depending on who you are as an investor. We see marketing materials all the time that tout the ability to invest only a few minutes per day yet still make very large returns, but the truth is just the opposite. Some investors quickly move from being a passive gold investor to an active trader because the market is interesting and the rewards can be significant, but this requires a lot of work.

Knowing what kind of investor you are will help you set realistic expectations about how much work will be required. For example, if you are interested in merely understanding how the gold market works and integrating a balanced gold position into your long-term diversified portfolio, you will find it relatively easy and the potential reward (based on long-term trends) should be satisfactory, though it will be lower than that of a more engaged (and therefore busier) trader. In the strategies section of the book we will spend time talking about these trade-offs with each example. This is all good news: The gold market is extremely flexible and liquid, and so it is reasonable to expect that you can design and execute trading or investing strategies that meet your risk tolerance and investing objectives. Because the gold market is unique and volatile, it may take practice and research regardless of your trading objectives, but anyone can do it.

Why Adequate Account Capitalization Is Important

Trading any asset requires capital that can be put at risk. That means that you are willing to lose money if things go bad in order to make profits when your forecast is correct. You certainly have heard the ubiquitous disclaimer that you should only risk capital that you (or your client) can afford to lose. Risking money that you need for debt payments, living expenses, education, or other necessities is a bad decision. Trading with an undercapitalized account (one that is full of money you "can't lose") invites emotional stress, and that always leads to very bad decision making. If you are unable to make rational decisions because you are stressed, you will be working against yourself and almost certainly will lose money.

This is an important concept to consider before entering the gold market. Unlike many other asset classes, gold is extremely easy to leverage. Some of the best ways to profit from gold are through futures and options, two types of instruments we will be spending a lot of time talking about in this book. However, traders can find themselves in a leverage trap when they treat it as a way to make bigger bets with a small account. If a small account is truly risk capital, this isn't a big deal, but if that small account is rent money, there will be a problem. There is no need to avoid the gold market if you have a small account. Your capital balance should be used to dictate risk tolerance and appropriate use of leverage, and as we discuss products and strategies, we will point out how leverage works in each case. Fortunately, gold investments can be used very effectively on an unleveraged basis, and so smaller traders still have all the flexibility they need.

Why Gold Traders Diversify

This book is not about why gold is the only asset you should be holding or trading. It is also not about why gold will beat stocks in the next decade or why gold should be held instead of a collapsing U.S. dollar. All those statements may turn out to be true, but we will be addressing why gold is an excellent addition to a well-diversified portfolio. That is true for long-term and short-term investors as well as very aggressive short-term traders. Having gold in your portfolio provides access to diversification that cannot be matched by other investment classes.

There are many ways to get gold exposure within your long- or short-term portfolio, and so matching your investment in gold to the other positions you currently hold or plan to hold is simple. The growing competition among modern gold investment products has driven costs so low that there is virtually no incremental disadvantage to splitting your exposure over a larger number of asset classes. Diversification works because each asset moves independently of the others. Gold, bonds, stocks, commodities, real estate, and other major asset classes rarely move in perfect correlation. That lack of correlation means that your total account has less risk than the weighted-average risk of each individual investment. Diversification is the only investment strategy we are aware of that reduces risk without unduly increasing costs or returns.

The counterargument to the benefits of diversification relies on the premise that because some asset classes will underperform others within a portfolio, there are significant opportunity costs. Of course, that argument relies on having perfect knowledge of performance in the past. Diversification is about the future and the unknowns we cannot predict. We hear that counterargument from serious gold bugs (investors dedicated exclusively to gold) all the time. Our response would be to consider the supposed opportunity costs they suffered in 2010 when they were invested in gold that made a measly 30 percent return while silver was up 70 percent. If gold had been priced in silver, it would have lost 25 percent of its value that year. A similar argument could be made for the superiority of residential real estate investing, which has outperformed gold despite the drawdowns of 2007 and 2008 over the last 15 years. These are extreme examples, but we think they make the point that it is just as unreasonable to allocate 100 percent of your assets to gold as it is to exclude gold entirely.

How to Avoid Excessive Costs

Gold can be one of the lowest-cost investments in your portfolio or can be the most expensive, depending on the choices you make as an investor. There are many different potential costs that gold investors have to watch out for, including excessive markups, expense ratios, wide spreads, illiquid funds, contango, commissions, and even dealers who trade against you. Some of these costs are very subtle and may be buried within dense disclosure documents or hidden completely. We will show you how to find those costs and make sure you are paying as little as possible.

This is important because costs are one of the few things over which investors have any control. We don't know what the future holds, but we do know how much we are paying in expenses and can do a lot to minimize those costs. We have seen many good traders make excellent timing decisions yet underperform passive indexes or even lose money over the long term because their costs were too high and they did not understand some of the hidden expenses that were leaching value from their accounts.

How to Reduce Trading Stress

Unlike income investments such as bonds and CDs, gold is not designed to deliver a payment stream, nor is it negotiable. Unlike stocks or many funds, it is not intentionally designed to rise in value over time. Gold may rise and it may fall, but there is no intent behind market participants (at least not usually) to increase its value. This is very different from stocks, in which a company's management team is specifically tasked with increasing shareholder value or a debt issuer who has an incentive to pay you back to retain his or her access to capital in the future. In this way gold is unique, and the market can be disorienting to new investors. This is important because the assumptions you would make about an investment in a stock or bond don't apply to gold, and if you are working with erroneous assumptions, it will create stress. We firmly believe that stress from your investing is an unnecessary complication to your life. If the stress from your investing activities is interfering with your overall happiness or other activities, it is a signal that there is something wrong with what you are doing.

The field of investor psychology often touches on the problems created by stress, and because it is subjective and thus varies from individual to individual, there are no clear rules for managing it. If it is too much for you to deal with and you are feeling unhappy, it is time to change, become more flexible, get some education, and reduce your financial exposure. Throughout this book we will provide examples of how investor stress affects central bankers, institutional investors, and individual traders and leads to bad decisions.

The good news is that the gold market is extremely flexible, and so adjustments are easy to make. In the book we will spend time discussing the strategies and products that can be the source of extreme stress for new investors and how to avoid them. We also will cover a spectrum of strategies that can ramp up the risk level but can be eased into slowly as you acquire more experience in the market.

How to Identify and Avoid Scams

The investing world is full of scams. Some are quite obvious get-rich-quick pitches, and others are more subtle and very difficult to identify. We can't explain why, but in our experience, next to the forex market, there are more scams centered on investing in gold than there are in any other investment class. Our hypothesis is that this is the case because gold investing is associated with fear and playing on fears or "selling pain" is an easy way to get traders to make bad decisions about their investing.

We will spend a little time on the subtle and not so subtle scams in the gold market in this book, but in general the following characteristics will tip you off before you get stuck.

- **Promises of unusually high returns.** If it sounds too good to be true, it is.
- **Proprietary or secret knowledge.** The great thing about the financial markets is transparency. It's not perfect, but for the most part you can assume that anything an advisor knows can be researched by you as well.

- **Alleged conspiracies.** These are used to create fear and explain why an advisor or scammer knows more about an investment than the public does.

It's easy to assume that scams are obvious like street vendors selling "genuine" Rolex watches on the streets of New York. However, in our experience the most dangerous scams are subtle and trap very sophisticated investors. Consider the 20+-year Ponzi scheme run by Bernie Madoff as an example of this kind of fraud. The scheme had all three of the characteristics outlined above, but Madoff toned it down so that it was easier for more experienced investors to believe (or want to believe).

Most of the scams in the gold market have more in common with Madoff's Ponzi scheme than they do with the fake watch salesmen. We can't detail every possible scam in the market, but we can help you understand the kinds of questions you should ask as you do your own research. You will learn that our definition of a scam includes several borderline-legal products that are probably the most difficult to identify. Be skeptical, ask questions, and demand proof. After all, whose money is at risk here?

Why Practice Really Does Make Perfect

We are writing this book with enough detail to be useful to traders who lack a strong background in the gold market. We have tried to emphasize practical applications and strategies over more political or historical information. That kind of content cannot be assimilated fully through reading alone but must be experienced so that you can learn from your mistakes. Throughout the book we will make specific suggestions for putting the concepts we discuss to the test in the live market. That experience is critical to becoming a successful participant in the gold market; however, investing with real money isn't for amateurs. If you want to be a better trader in the gold market, you can't just move your account to an active broker and start swinging for the fences, so before any new strategic idea is put into action, we strongly suggest that you practice in a paper account. It is easy to find resources for this kind of practice, and it can help you understand not only how a particular product or strategy works but how you feel about it as the market moves.

Practice is related to the myth of easy investing because it takes a lot of time and effort. Just as you would not expect to become a good guitar player by subscribing to a newsletter or magazine, you should not expect to become a good gold investor overnight. Because gold is so different from other markets, we can't stress enough the importance of doing research and investigation on your own before making any significant changes in your portfolio. If you plan to practice and investigate some of the more advanced ideas and strategies we will discuss, you will need a trading application designed to replicate the live market. You can access applications like that through the following links. We also have included some resources you can use to learn more about the basics of options and futures trading if you need a little extra background.

> **www.888options.com.** This site is supported and developed by the Options Industry Council, which is funded by the industry but has a surprisingly unbiased voice. Although the site promotes the use of options, we think the training materials, courses, Webinars, and research papers are realistic and useful. This site is pure education.

> **www.cboe.com.** The largest options exchange in North America, the Chicago Board Options Exchange (CBOE), maintains a crowded but useful site. They have three sponsored paper trading platforms for traders to use on an unlimited basis. You can find those under the "Tools" tab on the main page. CBOE also offers some good courses and a robust library of daily videos and Webinars.

> **www.optionshouse.com.** OptionsHouse is extremely competitive on price and specializes in active options

traders. They offer a paper trading account you can use
for a limited time that includes a very robust set of
analytical tools.

www.trademonster.com. Although a step up from
OptionsHouse in costs, TradeMonster does a great job of
helping traders understand and plan the trades they are
entering. The analytic tools are very robust and very easy
to use. This is ideal for a new active trader and can help
build a foundation of options knowledge before one
moves on to other platforms. TradeMonster also offers a
paper trading application.

Investing tools are becoming easier to use and more robust all
the time. There is a flood of excellent educational materials available about the gold market, options, and futures, and with a little
self-motivation there is no reason why you cannot become an
expert trader in the gold market. Whether you decide to use one
gold product exclusively or branch out and become strategically
diversified across gold ETFs, options, futures, and stocks, you can
find tools and analysis to help you make the most of your account;
best of all, most, if not all, of those tools are free or available at a
nominal cost.

How to Invest Profitably in the Gold Market

In the previous sections we concentrated on many of the things
that won't be included in the book, and we will end with the most
important thing that is included. We are big believers in tactical or
execution-based education, which means that we opted to skim
lightly over the obligatory chapters on gold's history, the gold standard, conspiracies, and politics. To be frank, it's just not that interesting, and it doesn't really help investors learn how to invest in
gold. There are plenty of great books that do a thorough job of covering those subjects if you are inclined to learn more.

In this book we will show you very specific and practical ideas for investing in gold. You can replicate what we have done easily and put it to the test. Because we can't cover every possible strategy, use the strategies that are included as a jumping-off point for learning more. If you need background information on some of the instruments and concepts that are beyond the scope of this book, you can find some recommended resources at the end.

CHAPTER 1

Gold Market
Background

We decided to stay fairly high-level in this section of the book so that we could concentrate on practical applications and investing strategies in the gold market. However, there are still a few things you need to understand about how gold is traded, who owns most of it, and why investors are so interested in the metal before you step into the market. Some of what you will learn will be a surprise and may motivate you to do some research on your own. There are some great resources for that kind of research, but be careful. The way gold is traded and priced today is very different from what it was at any time in the past.

Gold is traded by official (government or quasi-governmental) traders as well as the private sector and individuals. The official sector is many times larger than its private counterpart, but this kind of overlap is not unusual. Bonds, real estate, and commodities also are subject to massive interference from the official sector. However, unlike some of those other assets, gold is remarkably liquid and changes can be made much more quickly. Sometimes those changes can have a very material impact on prices; this is one of many reasons gold investors are so interested in monitoring the participants in the official sector.

Official and private gold investors trade in a few different markets. At the highest level most bullion is traded on the London Bullion Market by official traders (central banks mostly) and the largest international banks, some of which are referred to as bullion banks. Daily trading volume on the London Bullion Market is regularly equivalent to more than an entire year's worth of gold production, and many of the traders in the market are highly leveraged; this helps explain why the gold market can be so volatile.

Most private investors actually invest in gold through physical bullion (bar hoarding), but this is a very bullish and illiquid position for small traders. As a rule we suggest using exchange-traded products such as futures, options, and ETFs before beginning to buy physical bullion. Exchange-listed products have more flexibility, which is important for traders who are focused on strict money management and the benefits of diversification. The London Metals Exchange leads the world in gold derivatives trading, with the New York and Chicago futures and options exchanges right behind it in total volume. Exchange-traded funds (ETFs) are traded on the stock exchanges and are becoming more popular in the private sector. We see no signs that this interest will slow in the near term. For very small traders or long-term investors we feel that gold ETFs are probably the best way to access the gold market. In this book we will explain how to evaluate and invest in gold ETFs and how to use options on gold ETFs as a way to reduce volatility or gain additional leverage.

Besides knowing where gold is traded and how it trades, you will learn three basic things in the background section of the book. First, gold acts like a currency, and official and private investors treat it like one; that means it trends very differently than do other assets. As a currency, gold is "stateless," but it is influenced very heavily by the largest central banks in North America and Western Europe. Second, it is an extremely liquid market, which makes it very flexible and efficient. Liquidity is a big advantage for small traders and investors because it increases flexibility and keeps costs low. Third, gold and politics can be difficult to separate; this can be a hot button topic for many investors and analysts. This situation can be frustrating because political issues are emotionally charged and traders have to be unemotional about their investments to be able to make good decisions.

WHAT GOLD ISN'T

There are a lot of myths about gold, and it can be difficult for new investors to tell the difference between what is real and what isn't. In many cases myths are perpetuated as a way to create buying demand for gold investments, especially by gold bullion dealers, and we think it is important to consider the source when evaluating whether a particular statement about gold is true. The report you downloaded on the Internet or picked up at an investing trade show may be nothing more than a marketing piece for a bullion dealer.

The best myths are actually a mix of truth and speculation that lead to a conclusion that is either not true or impossible to prove. Others are entertaining examples of coincidences that have no relevance to today's market. Our challenge to you is to remain skeptical and do your own research to make sure you understand what you are getting into before you make a big financial decision. The following is a short list of our corrections to favorite myths that you should consider before jumping into the market. We start with those that are more of a misconception than a myth and end with those that are more troubling.

Gold Is Very Different from Stocks and Bonds

Gold is not like stocks and bonds, and it is different in some very important ways that should not be misunderstood. Gold often moves contrary to other major investment asset classes, but it can also unexpectedly become correlated with both stocks and bonds. For example, through the third quarter of 2010 stocks, bonds, and gold all began trending in the same direction. In fact, through most of the nascent economic recovery of 2009–2010 stocks, bonds, and gold moved the same way. This wasn't a problem for traders who happened to be long all three asset classes, but it raises questions about what would make them act like that and whether it represents a risk for gold investors.

Bonds are created to return value to investors. Debt pays interest and is designed to provide a return that is proportional to the risk the lender or investor is taking; therefore, the underlying purpose of a bond is to provide a return. Sounds obvious, we know, but this is a key differentiator between bonds and gold. Although it is technically possible to earn interest on certain gold deposits, gold does not return an income stream the way bonds do and probably never will. That means that gold will compete for investment capital with bonds when yields are high. That competition works against gold investors when yields are high and the economy is growing.

Stocks are actually quite similar to bonds in the sense that a share's price is equal to the discounted present value of its estimated future stream of payments (dividends). A company issues stock and proposes to investors willing to take a risk that the company has the ability to grow top-line revenue and bottom-line profits. Investors buy a stock because they believe that those future payments will return profits that are worth the risk they are taking. Because gold doesn't offer a meaningful income stream and isn't designed to grow in value, its trends are different from those of stocks. As you can imagine, because gold must compete for investment capital with stocks, it doesn't always do well in a bull market.

What you need to remember is that gold is not an investment that has been intentionally designed to go up or to create income for its investors. Over the very long term the purchasing power (value) of gold is "mean reverting," which means that it remains relatively flat. This is not a bad thing. Because of its ability to preserve value, gold is considered a good long-term store of value, and that is why it is such a good asset for account diversification. A store of value or safe-haven investment such as gold tends to perform poorly in an economic environment of high interest rates, strong economic growth, and relatively low inflation. The middle to late 1980s and the late 1990s were good examples of market conditions that hurt gold prices and helped other asset classes.

Gold Doesn't Act Like a Commodity

The problem here is that commodities are not just a homogeneous group of investments that rise and fall together at the same rate and the same time. Commodities fall into different categories, such as hard, soft, metals, precious metals, and energy, and each of those categories is sensitive to inflation, growth expectations, and global risks in different ways. Even within a specific class of commodities there will be differences. For example, from the time precious metals bottomed out after the market crash of 2008 until the end of 2010, silver prices had grown 226 percent but gold had rallied only 79.67 percent. In both cases, these gains are impressive, but they moved like that for different reasons. Gold and silver share some fundamental characteristics, but silver is much more sensitive to industrial demand than gold and therefore moves differently as a commodity.

The subsequent weak recovery in energy commodities through 2010 significantly underperformed gold, and that is not a surprise considering how different the underlying fundamentals are between gold and energy. This is one of the reasons we thought the fad of calling oil the "new gold" in 2007 was so ridiculous. The fact that one asset outpaces another for a brief period does not mean that one is taking the place of the other as a store of value or preferred investment. Much of the difference between gold and many commodities lies in the importance of gold as a currency or as backing (informal) for currencies. This is a point we will make several times in the book, and it is probably the most important characteristic new gold investors need to remember.

Gold Isn't Risk-Free

Although it is difficult to explain why gold is valuable and why it acts like a currency, we know that based on historical data, it provides significant benefits to short- and long-term investors. However, gold is not risk-free, and that is contrary to much of the advertising directed at potential investors. Gold has fallen in value in the past, and it seems likely that it will do so again at some point in the future. Imagine you had bought gold at the top of the market in 1980 and were still holding it 30 years later at the end of 2010. You would not have made any profits, and adjusted for inflation, you would still be in a losing position despite the recent bull market. There were a lot of buyers at the peak in 1980, and so this is a risk you need to consider as the market continues to rally. This isn't a problem exclusive to gold. It is an issue that traders in any market deal with and is something we will help you prepare for in your portfolio.

Short-term traders can be even more exposed to risk in the gold market because they tend to use leverage. Even a short-term retracement can be very damaging for an overleveraged investor. However, the fact that gold investing is risky is not bad news. If there were no risk in the market, there wouldn't be an opportunity to make profits either, and as a gold investor we are willing to take risks because we think there is significant upside potential. In the book we provide several specific examples of gold investing strategies, but we have made sure that the full risk and upside potential for each strategy are explained fully. A prepared investor is more likely to be flexible and productive over the long term. We have even included strategies that could be used to benefit investors if gold reenters an unexpected bear market.

THE MODERN HISTORY OF GOLD

Why is gold valuable? Although gold is a rare and useful element that has some industrial applications, demand from manufacturing is not likely to drive prices up or down very much.

Historically, gold has been used as money or as backing for paper money, but that model has largely been officially discarded by the world's major economies. Most gold produced each year is still used for jewelry, which could theoretically drive demand in good economic times, but that theoretical model hasn't been very predictive over the last few decades. As we have mentioned, gold also lacks an income stream like other investments, which could have driven its value. There must be something about what we have said that is not true because gold obviously has value and demand for the metal continues to grow. There are a lot of theories about this, but we think the most likely is that although it has been officially abandoned as currency, gold still acts like money.

Historically, gold is the most likely element to have been used as money. Gold is rare but can be found on the earth's surface; it's easy to refine and process at low temperatures; it doesn't tarnish, react, or dissolve; and it can't be consumed: It is probable that most of the gold that has ever been found is still with us in some form. Finally, gold is visually attractive and its purity is easy to determine. This combination of characteristics can't be found in any other element or precious metal. It is almost as though gold, as an element, was designed intentionally to be money. Gold's unique properties led to its use as a currency in the past, and that historical precedent may be the most important reason the metal is still used that way today.

This discussion about the mystery of gold's value is important because it can help traders both appreciate why gold is unique compared with other precious metals and avoid overconfidence in the factors that may drive gold's value in the future. Throughout the book we will stick with the theory that gold is valuable because it looks and acts like money. Figure 1-1 shows how gold prices have reacted to the value of the dollar versus a basket of other global currencies over the last 30 years, since gold began to float more freely against the U.S. dollar. The strong inverse relationship

FIGURE 1-1

Spot gold prices versus U.S. dollar index values, January
1980–December 2010.

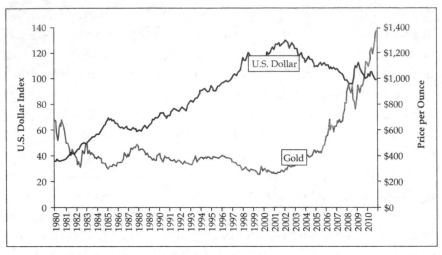

Source: World Gold Council/U.S. Federal Reserve

shown in the figure occurred because the U.S. dollar is the world's
reserve currency, and we will demonstrate that it is backed by gold
(officially or not). This model will help provide important context
for why traders drive prices up during times of uncertainty and
what factors may lead to a future decline.

How Did Gold Get to This Point?
A Short History Lesson

We won't go into too much detail about the long history of gold
here, but we think that a brief discussion of the major events in the
gold market over the last three centuries will help explain why it
was used as a currency and how that legacy remains. Our second
objective here is to explain where the major players in the gold
market came from and provide a little of the context for some of
their activities.

1717

Isaac Newton set the official price of gold at 4.25 British pounds. This was one of many attempts to fix the price of gold, something that has been attempted several times since then and is usually wildly unsuccessful.

1900

Gold was adopted as the single metallic standard for U.S. money. The original standards of one dollar to the Mexican peso or a fixed amount of silver (how times change) were abandoned.

1933

During the Depression, President Roosevelt banned gold exporting and put a stop to the convertibility of paper into gold. He also outlawed holding gold as an investment and ordered U.S. citizens to turn in the excess gold they owned to the U.S. government. This was not the first time this kind of action had been taken, and the United States was not the only country to do so during the Depression.

Another way to look at this event is to consider that the gold standard created a risk of speculative attacks on the sovereign currency (which happened) and prevented the government from expanding the money supply and avoid rapid deflation. By ending convertibility, world governments were not as constrained and could increase the money supply beyond the gold standard's limits. Whether this was a good thing probably depends on the time frame. The consensus among many economists is that the earlier an economy abandoned the gold standard and inflated its money supply, the earlier it emerged from the Great Depression. That single observation (true or not) has been the root of much of the intellectual reasoning behind the current campaign to inflate the money supply in the United States. Although the events of 1933 are much debated, they are extremely important. It is one of the most important modern examples illustrating the relationship money has with gold and the futility of attempting to fix the value of any asset indefinitely. When investors lose confidence in a currency, gold can serve as an alternative, and rising demand for gold as a store of value will increase its price (eventually) regardless of the actions of the government.

1973

The United States officially ended the gold standard and allowed both the dollar and gold to float freely. The ban on ownership of gold as an investment also was lifted. Since that time the value of gold versus the dollar (like any currency exchange rate) has moved up and down as investors have grown fearful (rising gold prices) or more confident (falling gold prices) about the economy.

1980

Gold prices hit an all-time high of $870 per ounce. The price of gold in inflation-adjusted dollars has never been higher than it was in 1980. It is not a coincidence that this historic price spike 30 years ago occurred during a recession that was accompanied by excessive price inflation and war in the Middle East. A lack of confidence in the U.S. dollar's value probably contributed to the spike in gold prices as gold was sought out as a store of value.

It is even more important to think about what happened next, from 1980 to the early 2000s, when gold entered a prolonged bear market. Higher interest rates and a bubble in the precious metals markets that hurt investor confidence both contributed to the decline. The important thing to remember here is that gold does not always go up in price; however, this does not mean that investors can't profit just as effectively in a bear market as they can in a gold bull market.

1997 and 1999

The U.S. government approved gold as an asset that could be held in an individual retirement account (1997), and 15 of the largest central banks in the world signed an agreement to limit annual gold sales. The combined effect of these two events can be seen in the subsequent introduction of better gold investing products and renewed interest in gold as a store of value. Smaller investors could more easily hold gold as an asset in their portfolios, and central banks were providing underlying support for prices. The net effect has been an incredible rally in gold prices since the early 2000s.

We expect to see the pressure from new gold investors and central banks that need to acquire gold as a reserve to continue putting bullish pressure on the market. This doesn't mean that there won't be volatility, but we believe it will create a situation in which buying on support will be very profitable. In the strategy sections we will go into much more detail about investing in favor of the trend and how to identify those potential support levels by using analysis.

2008–2011
The underlying pressure of new buyers and central banks combined with the market disruptions of the "Great Recession" will push gold prices to all-time highs as measured in absolute dollar terms and eventually in inflation-adjusted prices as well. The effects of the Federal Reserve's global campaign of quantitative easing during this period are uncertain, but it seems likely that the expansion of the U.S. money supply is contributing to the rise in gold prices because investors are fearful that the expansion of the money supply will lead to a decline in the dollar's purchasing power.

2011 and Beyond
As one of the few realistic alternatives to the U.S. dollar as a reserve or safe-haven investment, gold is important to investors and central banks, many of which have very limited exposure to gold and are overweight in the U.S. dollar. Asian central banks in particular are too concentrated in U.S. dollar assets and need to diversify into gold as a reserve asset. That kind of buying could have a very positive effect on the price of gold.

ECONOPOLITICS OF GOLD

To attempt a discussion of the role of gold in politics and government is to enter very deep waters. However, this is an unavoidable necessity for new traders because the official sector plays such a large role in the gold market. Although most economies have moved off an official gold standard, they still hold gold as a reserve asset directly or hold it indirectly by investing in currencies such as the U.S. dollar and the euro. There is a legitimate argument to be made that although gold doesn't have a fixed relationship to currencies anymore, we are still on a gold standard. If you are interested in learning more about that theory, we would suggest starting with the Real Bills Doctrine as a way to learn more about reserve banking and its relationship to gold deposits.

When we discuss gold in the official sector, we encourage you not to think about those actions in terms of good and bad but to consider how those actions affect your portfolio holdings. As we mentioned before, you may disagree with current monetary and fiscal policies in the United States, Europe, and China, but you can't afford to sacrifice your profitability in order to feel vindicated. In this section we will discuss the econopolitical role gold plays in the official sector from the perspective of gold's price trend. Putting the official sector's behavior in the context of the trend will be a useful tool for separating yourself from the emotional aspects of politics.

Why Was It a Gold Standard?

The gold standard can mean different things, but it usually refers to a currency backed by gold bullion. This means that the central monetary authority such as the government or a central quasi-governmental entity such as the U.S. Federal Reserve issues currency (paper and coins) that is fully backed by gold bullion that the government or central bank owns. Usually in a gold standard (but not always) the currency is also exchangeable for physical gold bullion. With a gold standard, the currency in circulation is more or less fixed to a certain quantity of gold bullion; theoretically, this means that the money supply is difficult to expand and therefore value is more durable. A gold standard is also supposed to increase confidence in the currency and monetary system because the population knows that there is a real asset backing the value of the currency.

Confidence is the real objective behind a gold standard, and we will show that when confidence is high, gold tends to trend flat or even down, whereas it goes up when confidence is low. In a way, a reinstated gold standard would be a bad thing for gold investors hoping to make money from big moves in the gold market. When done correctly, a gold standard should reduce volatility in the market, and that makes profits a little harder to earn. In the past there have been several different versions of the gold standard or partial gold standards that have been attempted. For example, during the 1930s the U.S. Federal Reserve had to back at least 40 percent of the money supply with gold bullion, which was a partial standard. One consequence of that partial standard was that the money supply could not be expanded to reduce interest rates and avoid deflation during the Great Depression. At the same time other economies, such as France, were hoarding gold, which further compounded the issues faced in the United States.

You don't need to be an economic expert to do a little reading on how and why the gold standard has been deployed over the last 200 years and why it has always failed. You will learn that it has its own problems and is prone to collapse when the need for spending exceeds the government's access to gold bullion. The two most common causes of this condition are war and extreme financial crises.

However, not having a gold standard poses extreme risks of its own. One frequently cited case of the dangers of leaving a gold standard is post–World War I Germany. The German Treasury was already depleted of gold after funding the war and making reparation payments in gold or foreign currency forced the German government to move to a fully fiat (no backing) currency system to fund payments. The problem was that spending had to increase while income was shrinking, which led to a catastrophic economic collapse. Although the current situation in the United States and Europe is not as extreme as this, it should still sound familiar.

Because the Germans had to make massive annual payments for reparations, they attempted to back their purchases of foreign currency with government debt. This is often called debt monetization, and it led to a crash in confidence. Ultimately the German currency fell from 60 marks to the U.S. dollar to essentially being worthless, and at the end German banks turned over the old marks to junk dealers to be recycled as paper. The unbacked paper currency and debt issued by the German government led to hyperinflation in the 1920s and probably contributed to the political instability that allowed the Nazi party to come to power. Although we have mentioned reparations as a potential cause of the crash, there were many other factors. Widespread labor strikes that the government supported, a flight of capital (including gold) to more stable economies, French and Allied occupation forces installed across the country, and the ongoing threat of war also contributed to the real cause of hyperinflation and economic collapse: fear.

What causes a lack of confidence in or extreme fear about a currency can vary, and ultimately these factors are probably only partially understood in the past tense. It usually manifests itself as extreme inflation because the currency is being discounted for uncertainty. These confidence crises have occurred around the world for many different underlying reasons. For example, in the 1940s the Hungarians went through a period of hyperinflation that peaked at an inflation rate of $1.3 \times 1,016$ percent. You know that things are getting bad when you have to describe your inflation rate in exponential terms. During hyperinflation normal monetary tools are no longer effective. It is unreasonable to assume that anything other than very extreme policies, regime changes, or a new monetary system will be able to fix the issues once hyperinflation takes hold. This brings us full circle to the original topic of this section: A gold standard should help stabilize confidence in the currency, and without it fear can lead to volatility and panic in the currency market.

We are not predicting that inflationary cycles like those during the last century in Germany and Hungary will occur in the United States and Europe in the near future, but we are convinced that confidence in currency is likely to continue falling, which will be supportive for a bullish trend in gold. We think that reinstating the gold standard in any major global economy is unlikely, and so volatility is going to be the norm rather than the exception, and that will present opportunities for gold investors who are willing to take some risk. If we assume that there is no way to return to the gold standard and that the major economies of the world will maintain the kinds of extreme measures they have taken recently, we expect gold to still be one of the best returning assets in the market over the next five years. The issue of confidence is important, and it doesn't require a full collapse of the economy to initiate an extension of the current bull trend in gold.

What Is a Fiat Currency, and Is It a Bad Thing?

We have already referred to currency systems in Europe, the United States, and most of Asia as fiat currency systems; this means that the government issues money that represents value and is negotiable but is not backed by any real asset. Essentially a fiat currency is backed by the good faith of the government that issues it, and that is a very difficult concept for many investors to understand. How could a currency that has no intrinsic worth be valuable? It is difficult to understand why a government would want a fiat currency. It seems that there is a huge risk of a large segment of the population waking up and realizing that the money in their savings accounts is just a bunch of worthless paper. We have yet to find satisfactory reasons as to why that kind of panic doesn't happen, but there is no shortage of theories. It is also worth noting that a fiat currency system can exist under a gold standard when the value of the currency doesn't match the value of the underlying gold. This was the situation in the United States for a long time before President Richard Nixon officially ended the gold standard in the 1970s.

Fiat money introduces special risks into a currency system. Because the U.S. dollar is a fiat currency, the Federal Reserve can increase the supply of money by buying debt from the Treasury and on the open market without any limits. When it does that, it creates money on its balance sheet that is essentially a liability for the Fed. The Fed theoretically can increase the money supply indefinitely, which leverages the Fed's balance sheet. A universal law about the market is that leverage increases risk because the more leveraged you are as an investor, the less flexible you become. A fiat currency can give the government the ability to meet financing needs that are beyond its assets and income for a short time. However, the ability to leverage the currency increases risk, and during a crisis investors can lose confidence. The salient point here for gold investors is that under a fiat currency system a crisis is likely to drive a bullish trend in gold. The reverse is also true when the economy is growing and confidence increases. Investors are more willing to take on risk in a growing economy, and gold will often become less desirable.

Therefore, a fiat system can be good and bad for gold investors. The fact that a currency isn't backed by an asset doesn't mean that it won't appreciate in value against gold in good economic times. This is often confusing to investors, who correctly assume that a fiat currency is still very likely to inflate or lose value year over year regardless of a good or bad economy. They may be tempted to infer incorrectly that gold therefore should rise in value. Gold can actually be a pretty poor hedge against an inflating fiat currency during good economic times. When we cover the fundamentals of the gold market, we will provide more detail about when and how to use gold as an inflation hedge. There are times when the inflation of a fiat currency will get out of control regardless of whether the underlying economy is growing, and gold tends to do very well in those conditions.

Why Not Return to a Gold Standard?

The disadvantages of an unbacked and fully fiat currency are obvious. Governments and central banks don't have a great track record for exercising self-control during a crisis. Printing electronic money the way the Fed did during the 2008–2010 financial crisis created a big risk that will be difficult to unwind. Even if a return to a gold standard was a panacea that could cure the global debt, inflation, and liquidity problems we continue to deal with in 2011, there is a key complication standing in the way of a return to a metallic standard.

Gold supplies and production are not evenly distributed around the globe. New supplies are not very flexible, and mining is concentrated in just a few places. Production constraints can lead to their own brand of bubbles and crashes. Gold mining itself is heavily concentrated in China, the United States, South Africa, Australia, and Russia, in that order. If it is true that gold production rates can be a constraint on growth, would any government be willing to hand over monetary policy to the Russian and Chinese governments? In addition to the sovereign independence issues, private gold mining companies are massive and could exert a lot of control over production. Barrick Gold Corporation (ABX), the world's largest gold miner, produced 2.06 million ounces of gold in the third quarter of 2010.[1] On an annualized basis, that is approximately 10 percent of total global mining production in 2009 from a single company.[2]

---

[1] Barrick Gold Earnings Call Transcript, Q3 2010 results.
[2] World Gold Council, 2nd Quarter Gold Supply Report.

We could go into much more detail about these issues and why they are difficult to solve, but the issue here is not whether a return to the gold standard is a good idea or even necessary. We just want to provide an explanation for why the status quo of fiat currencies and a semi-independent gold market is likely to persist. This is a good thing for us as gold investors because more government intervention would not be a good thing for gold prices.

CHAPTER 2

The Major Players

There are several major players in the market, and the large investors you will learn about in this chapter can exert an extraordinary influence on prices; therefore, it is necessary to understand who they are and what motivates them to make changes in their portfolio positions. Most of the time, the major investors in the gold market move very slowly, and that is good for trend traders looking for an opportunity to ride the wave created by the big money.

We will divide the major players in the gold market into three main groups:

1. The official sector, including central banks, the International Monetary Fund (IMF), and other government entities.

2. Institutional investors and funds, including ETFs, hedge funds, bullion banks, and other large private investors.

3. Gold producers may overlap with the other two categories, but here we are referring to private firms involved in gold mining, exploration, and refining.

THE FED'S RELATIONSHIP TO GOLD

The Federal Reserve, like most central banks, maintains capital reserves to back its liabilities. These reserves or assets are shown on the balance sheet, which is available on the Fed's Web site each week. These reserves can be in the form of foreign currencies or gold, among other assets. Gold reserves can be lent for income and used for settlement of international transactions. However, the primary purpose of these gold reserves is similar to the purpose they serve for a long-term individual investor who is using gold to diversify her portfolio: Gold is a store of value and represents an asset that can be used to boost confidence in the money supply or to execute monetary policy when necessary.

Officially, the U.S. central bank holds 8,133 tonnes[1] of gold, which is roughly equal to 5 percent of all the gold that has ever been mined.[2] That is an astounding figure when one considers that it is very probable that all or most of the gold that has ever been mined is still with us in one form or another. No other single entity comes close to this level of gold ownership, and this is one of the reasons we still insist that the U.S. dollar is essentially backed by gold even though the relationship isn't fixed.

The relationship that the U.S. central bank has with gold has changed over time. When the nation was on the gold standard, the central bank could only issue currency equal to or at a fixed ratio to the total value of the gold in its vaults. That constraint combined with arbitrary values set on gold made things very difficult for the U.S. central bank during times of crisis. For example, during the Great Depression the U.S. central bank had to back at least 40 percent of the money supply with gold that it owned. This fixed rela-

---

[1] Large investors, including central banks, trade gold in *tonnes*, which is sometimes called a metric ton in North America. A tonne is equal to 1,000 kilograms or roughly 2,200 pounds. Because gold traders use the term *tonne*, we will do that throughout this book as well.

[2] World Gold Council, "World of Gold Report."

tionship between gold and the central bank's ability to grow or shrink the money supply was one of the key factors many economists blame for the severity and length of the Great Depression. Ben Bernanke, the current chairman of the Federal Reserve, made this argument well before the market crash of 2007–2008. He vowed not to allow anything to stop the Federal Reserve from increasing the money supply during the next liquidity crisis.

True to his word, the current Federal Reserve has not allowed the fixed amount of gold currently held in reserve to prevent it from issuing a new money supply to bank reserves through several rounds of "quantitative easing." At the time of this writing, excess reserves held by banks in the United States have come down slightly but are still close to $1 trillion. Keep in mind that since the 1960s this number has remained very close to zero dollars.[3]

The relationship that the Federal Reserve has with gold has changed from time to time, but we suggest that the most fundamental shift took place in 1971 during the "Nixon shock." During that period, the U.S. government made some attempts at price and wage fixing and ended the convertibility of dollars to gold. Looking back on that action, it is amazing that the U.S. dollar did not suffer a more serious value crisis in the subsequent decade than it did. At the time, the U.S. government was able to use the threat of war and the central banks of France, West Germany, and Switzerland as scapegoats for its own problems. Shifting the blame like that probably helped prevent a more serious speculative attack on the U.S. dollar. The end result of that action, which is often referred to as "closing the gold window," was to force the major currencies in the world into a full floating system. There were some attempts to manage currencies within trading bands and other fixed relationships, but almost all of them failed.

Representing the largest economy in the world, in 1971 the Federal Reserve pulled off quite a coup by replacing gold with the

---

[3] Federal Reserve Bank of St. Louis, "Excess Reserves of Depository Institutions."

dollar as the most important reserve asset in the world. Since that time, many large central banks have held the dollar as their most significant asset and some central banks, including those of India and China, have concentrated almost all their reserves in U.S. dollars. This is a benefit for the United States because it is now in the best interest of the world's largest economies to maintain the strength and stability of the U.S. economy and currency. The shift away from a partial gold standard carries special risks. On the one hand, the Federal Reserve can "print" or create as much money as it wishes to provide flexibility and bailouts during times of crisis, but on the other hand, the electronic printing press can be run too much, which could cause investors to lose confidence in the U.S. dollar, after which inflation could accelerate out of control.

In theory, flexibility sounds good; however, in the real world, extreme monetary policies create many unknowns. For such an expansion of the monetary supply in bank reserves to be a good thing, the future effects of those policies would have to be known. Since the future cannot be known, the Federal Reserve is taking a significant gamble. This is one of the reasons investors have found gold so attractive over the last few years. If the Federal Reserve winds up being wrong (not a certainty) about the future repercussions of its actions, the U.S. dollar could fall dramatically. As a store of value, gold should provide some protection against those losses for both the Federal Reserve and individual investors.

It doesn't take an economist to understand why the Federal Reserve could be wrong about its actions. Look at it this way: If economic forecasting was reliably accurate, why didn't the economists at the Federal Reserve see the crisis of 2007–2008 coming before it was upon us? The answer is that they couldn't, which is why so many traders (including the authors) are building investing plans to hedge against or even profit from the inability to predict the future. To a great extent the current money-printing campaign by the Federal Reserve is based on ideas that weren't implemented during the Great Depression but in theory might have helped.

Expanding the money supply might have helped the United States in the 1930s, but we will never know. Arguably, it could have exacerbated speculative attacks on the U.S. dollar and made the situation much worse. However, the choice has been made, and the Federal Reserve is injecting trillions of dollars into the economy to try to head off a Great Depression–style liquidity trap and deflation. It can do this because the dollar is no longer backed in any way by gold . . . or is it?

The complete abandonment of gold in the 1970s as a backing for currency changed the relationship the government has with gold, but if the U.S. dollar is backed solely by confidence in the economy and the good faith of the U.S. government, why does the Federal Reserve still need any gold on the balance sheet? This is an important question because it gets to the heart of why individual investors should have gold on their own balance sheets. We will dig into the answer to this question next and will show that the central bank in the United States needs to hold gold and that central banks that don't are likely to change direction and begin acquiring the asset in the near future. We suspect that even if the current crisis begins to ease in 2011 and 2012, there will still be bullish pressure on the gold market as these goldless central banks begin to diversify their reserve holdings away from the U.S. dollar and into gold among other assets. That is a good thing for investors.

There are three primary reasons why a central bank should hold a large position in gold as a reserve asset.

Risk Diversification

The basic premise of diversification is that when uncorrelated assets are combined into a single portfolio, the average risk will be lower than that of any single asset class within the portfolio. Gold is one of several asset classes that can be included in a portfolio to achieve adequate diversification. The way this applies to individual investors is not much different from the way it applies to central banks. Central banks are just like us in that they don't want the value of their reserves to shrink unexpectedly. If their reserves are concentrated in U.S. dollar and euro holdings (which almost all of them are), they are exposed to considerable risks when large unexpected events such as the 2007–2010 U.S. financial crisis occur. Gold is suitable for diversification at the official level because it is one of the largest and most liquid financial markets. Besides other currencies and sovereign debt, gold is one of the few assets that are large enough to be effective at that level while still being relatively free from political conflicts of interest.

Central banks periodically sell or acquire gold the way an individual does, but historically they tend to do this at the worst possible times because, like individual investors, they are return chasers. What that means is that when times are good and global currencies are strong, gold often falls in value and central banks are tempted to sell their losing positions in gold and jump into more attractive assets. Similarly, when times are bad and the future of the U.S. dollar, the yen, or the euro is in doubt, central bankers come under significant pressure to acquire gold and diversify. One of the many dilemmas that investors (including central bankers) face is that it is easy and cheap to diversify when times are good and you "don't need it" but it becomes much more expensive and controversial to do so when you actually are in need of protection.

Although central bankers like to think of themselves as conservative and rational, their recent track record suggests otherwise. This problem may not be all bad for individual gold investors because diversification at the official level would create long-term support for gold prices. This is certainly not a new idea. Over the last several years, more central banks have been threatening to diversify beyond the dollar. Russia, China, and India are three of the largest emerging markets to have made public statements to that effect recently. Although they haven't made much progress yet, it seems likely that they have learned a very hard lesson over the last three or four years. Even if only a few of them began making changes in earnest, it would have a profound impact on the price of gold as they built more diversified reserves.

Economic Independence

Unlike the U.S. dollar, gold is not issued by a government and its value cannot be changed permanently by rivals or allies. If you want stability and immunity from the actions of third parties, gold cannot be beat, whereas holding sovereign debt or foreign currencies makes central banks dependent on a third party to preserve and maintain the value of those assets. Consider the current relationship between the Chinese and U.S. governments. The United States is continuing to issue massive amounts of debt into the market to raise capital for deficits and execute monetary policies such as quantitative easing. The Chinese have been quite eager to be a buyer of much of that debt, which is now north of $1 trillion. That is a big debt by any measure, and it is common for political commentators to describe this situation as though the United States were at the mercy of the Chinese, the country's largest creditor. However, this is not exactly true. Instead, the Chinese are quite dependent on the United States to maintain the value of those assets. That means that the Chinese are dependent on U.S. policy makers and the Federal Reserve and have limited control over this massive "asset."

It is possible that the Chinese could decide to sell their U.S. debt that is held as a reserve asset, but if they did that, very quickly the price of that debt could fall precipitously, which would drive down the value of their reserves. This is a problem because the Chinese already are dealing with serious and potentially dangerous levels of inflation, and prices in China could quickly begin rising out of control if investors lost faith in the Chinese currency because its reserves were in danger.

The Chinese government has a concentrated risk in U.S. Treasuries, which means that if U.S. debt falls too much, it will take the central bank with it. The bottom line is that the Chinese do not have the independence they need. This risk must be diversified, and unfortunately for them, that means they have to play the role of supplicant in the short term to their largest customer and borrower: the U.S. economy. We recognize that this is a controversial subject, but whether you feel that the Chinese have the upper hand or the United States does, the bottom line is good for gold investors. We are sure most traders and analysts would agree that the relationship between China and the United States is dysfunctional at best and that something will have to change if independence is to be maintained. That probably means diversification (sensing a theme here?), in which case gold will be in greater demand as a reserve asset.

A Protective Put

A protective put is an option that an investor may apply against a specific long position or against an overall bullish bias in his portfolio. The protective put acts like an insurance policy that will protect the investor against large losses. For example, imagine that you own XYZ stock that is priced at $100 but the company's earnings announcement is on the horizon and you are concerned that it will disappoint investors. If it turns out to be a big earnings miss, the stock could drop 20 to 50 percent in a single day. If you own a protective put on the same stock, the put will gain in value as the stock drops, which will offset most of those losses. As you can imagine, a protective put isn't free. It's a lot like an insurance policy against catastrophic loss, and that requires an investment.

A central bank will invest in gold for the same reasons a stock investor will buy a protective put: as insurance against rare but catastrophic losses. For example, a strong position in gold will gain in value as its currency drops and is still negotiable for international transactions if the currency experiences a speculative attack. A central bank hopes that emergencies like this never happen and that the gold it is holding never will be needed in that way; however, like fires or accidents, these unexpected events tend to be rare, dramatic, disruptive, and impossible to predict. They could include war, an unexpected surge in inflation, and trade conflicts with major partners. These all qualify as rare and unlikely, but when they do happen, it's good to have a hedge.

India had to turn to gold to survive an economic crisis in 1991. A combination of massive deficit spending, slowing exports, and a struggling economy contributed to the crisis, and as the Indian government tried to spend its way out of trouble, investors began leaving the country and dumping its currency. India was experiencing a crisis of confidence and could have suffered complete economic collapse. In an attempt to head off disaster the government was able to negotiate a loan of $2.2 billion from the IMF and Japan that was secured against 47 tonnes of its gold reserves, which was physically flown to the Bank of England for safekeeping. That collateral was equal to 70 percent of the total gold holdings of the Indian government. Can you imagine what could have happened if this had not worked? It was fortunate for India that it had the gold available for this loan, but it was only enough for one round of financing. Ultimately this story has a moderately positive ending: The government changed hands, and reforms were instituted. Although the disruption was significant, it was not enough to bring about a full collapse because the central bank had access to gold—its emergency protective put.

One of the key factors that led to the crisis was a massive current account (trade) deficit and unsustainable government spending. What other economies can you think of that run massive trade deficits and spend much more than they receive in revenues? What happened to India will happen again, and if investors have a crisis of confidence in the U.S. dollar, the U.S. Federal Reserve has access to gold that should help maintain some of its value in a crisis. Although a protective put can't protect against all losses, it may be enough to stave off complete disaster. The list of unknown events that could cause a crisis like this is long and justifies an expensive but necessary holding in gold. As global growth continues and more economies realize they need protection from the big unknowns, we believe that situation will push demand for gold. This is a fundamental trend that long-term investors can take advantage of through a partial portfolio allocation in precious metals.

CENTRAL BANKS

We have discussed the reasons why a central bank should hold gold as a reserve asset and why some banks in emerging markets are likely to add gold reserves in the future. However, central banks are not just gold buyers; they can also be very large gold sellers. Although no one seems to be doing much selling now, this could be a big issue for traders who are trying to forecast the potential impact of the proverbial 900-pound gorillas in the market.

Besides the United States and the IMF, the other gold gorillas are concentrated in Western Europe and the United Kingdom. When combined, the gold reserves of Germany, France, and Italy exceed those of the United States, and if you add Switzerland, Netherlands, the European Central Bank (ECB), Portugal, and the United Kingdom, they exceed both the United States' and the IMF's gold reserves put together. There is a long list of other major central banks with smaller holdings, and any of them could become a net seller, effectively flooding the market and depressing prices. This is not a problem only for traders trying to forecast the strength of gold's trend; other central banks are concerned about this risk as well. Unlike profit-seeking investors, central banks often conduct market activities for political reasons, which are difficult to understand and predict. To solve this problem, at least partially, many of the major central banks have created agreements detailing how much gold they will sell and when they will sell it. Those agreements are shared with the market, and so there is a certain level of transparency.

The most important of the agreements currently in place is known as the third Central Bank Gold Agreement, which covers the central banks in the European Union, Sweden, Switzerland, and the IMF. The agreement, which is in place until 2014, set a maximum annual sales pace of 400 tonnes of gold from the participating central banks. The objective of the agreement was to make sure that the market can absorb and plan for the supply of gold coming from those banks without experiencing big price disruptions. It's very interesting to see how the central banks changed their attitudes toward gold selling as the credit crisis of 2007–2008 emerged and then got worse over the next two years. Under this agreement (and two prior agreements) gold selling started off at 400 tonnes in 1999 and spiked to 497 tonnes in 2004 (the annual limit at the time was 500 tonnes) but dropped to 20 tonnes in 2010. We don't have the final number from 2010 yet, but it seems unlikely to be much larger than the original estimates.

This agreement raises two questions. First, why did central banks want to sell gold a decade ago but now do not, and second, why did they need an agreement in the first place? The answer to the first question is that central bankers are a lot like bad individual investors; they sell investments at the bottom of the market and buy (or hold) at the top of the market. The liquidity crisis changed investors' attitudes about gold as a store of value, and central bankers are no different from investors.

The second question is more interesting. The agreement was needed because the banks were dumping gold onto the market and prices were falling fast. This was not good for the banks that still felt gold was a necessary reserve asset, and it could have been destabilizing to private enterprises (such as big banks) that held massive positions in gold. It was in their combined best interest to prevent a selling frenzy from hitting the market. At the time, the best they could do was agree to a maximum sales volume and communicate that plan to the market. Whether that did very much to stabilize the market is uncertain, but it seems like more than a coincidence that the original agreement coincided with a 20-year low in gold prices and the end of the gold bear market. The agreement also coincided with a strategic decision by the U.S. Federal Reserve to lower the value of the U.S. dollar on the international market, and those two factors combined to form perfect market conditions for a long-term gold rally.

The bottom line for gold investors is that the gold market has some risk overhang in the form of massive potential sellers. We believe that economic conditions over the next 10 to 20 years will be such that a large reserve position will be an absolute requirement to preserve confidence in a currency, but the unexpected can happen. Gold traders should pay attention to the big official investors and learn why and how they buy and sell.

THE IMF

Surprisingly, the International Monetary Fund comes just behind the United States and Germany and just before France and Italy as the third largest gold investor in the world. The IMF has several missions, but a few of the most important are to support international exchange rates, make loans to struggling economies, and stabilize international markets. We think this mission could be summarized as follows: The IMF's mission is to restore or create confidence. We won't comment on whether that can actually be done through artificial intervention—oops, we just did.

Our argument so far in this book is that a large position in gold reserves is positively correlated with higher confidence levels in a currency. When the IMF was formed in 1944, the gold standard was common. The initial members of the IMF were required to contribute annual dues in the form of gold, and as the IMF's membership has grown, its assets have grown as well. However, gold is not an income producer until you sell it, and in April 2008 the IMF approved the sale of one-eighth of its gold holdings, or approximately 400 tonnes, to fund continued operations. So far, those sales have been to other official sector (central banks) participants, and so there hasn't been a big change in the balance among the major players in the gold market. Transferring gold this way may not have increased supply, but it did destroy some demand, and so the impact is still something we are concerned about.

The IMF planned to avoid unduly disrupting the gold market by making sure that its sales would fall within the limit of 400 tonnes per year set by the big European central banks and by marketing the gold to other official sector investors before trying to sell it to private investors. It has promised to report gold sales as quickly as possible to keep other market participants informed, and so far a little more than half of this gold has been sold to official buyers (mostly India). In 2010 the IMF announced that it would begin selling the other half on the open market with the goal of using the proceeds to fund its lending activities and attempt to diversify its own assets. Don't make the mistake of assuming that the IMF today is the same as the IMF of 1944 or 1980 or 1990. Its policies change dramatically over time, and from time to time the IMF has been a massive gold seller. From 1976 to 1980 the IMF sold off one-third of its gold assets to its members for $35 an ounce. We wouldn't say that the IMF is a wild card in the gold market, but the relationship the organization has with its members and other market participants is a little weird. This means that the strategy currently in place could change and cause a disruption in prices.

As we have mentioned, this change in the IMF's gold owner-ship is part of a new funding strategy. The fund can't sustain itself on income from lending because it makes loans to bad risks; that seems like a strange thing to do, but it is part of the IMF's mandate and purpose. The new income strategy is to sell the gold and invest the proceeds in growing mature economies for profits that will support the fund's operations and replace the losses from loans it makes to bad economies. Currently the IMF has about 1.3 billion

SDRs[4] that are in arrears from countries to which it has made loans, so we hope its investing activities are very successful.

So far, we haven't seen big problems emerge from the implementation of this strategy because there has been excess demand in the market over the last few years that has supported gold prices and because the IMF has been buying massive amounts of short-term U.S., euro zone, and Japanese government bonds with the proceeds. This is a great investing strategy when bonds are in a massive asset bubble (2008–2010), but if it pops, the IMF will have problems. Our point here is not to criticize the IMF (that would be too easy); it is to make sure you understand another source of risk overhang in the gold market. The IMF probably will need to sell more gold in the future and official buyers may not be available, and so the market will have to step up. That increase in supply could have a short-term bearish impact on gold prices.

This doesn't mean that gold prices definitely will fall when the IMF needs to sell more; it just means that the potential is there for a disruption and gold investors will need to be flexible. We think that demand will be great enough over the next decade to absorb a lot of gold selling by the IMF, but it is better to know the risks before they become an issue. At this point we think it is safe to assume that the IMF will be communicative enough for gold investors to anticipate its plans in advance.

ETFs AND GOLD FUNDS

Gold investment funds and ETFs are very large, and although they don't generally acquire or sell gold very quickly, they are a major player in the market. To get some perspective, consider that at the end of 2010 the U.S. Treasury was holding just under 8,133 tonnes of gold and the SPDR Gold Shares ETF (GLD) held 1,299 tonnes. In

---

[4] SDRs (Special Drawing Rights) are a special currency the IMF uses to make loans. That amount is roughly equal to $2 billion in U.S. dollars.

other words, one ETF's gold holdings equaled 16 percent of the total gold holdings of the U.S. Treasury. GLD is the largest ETF or fund of its kind and is one of the investment alternatives we will discuss in this book. There are other funds that invest in gold bullion the way GLD does, but they are nowhere near its size. For example, iShares has an ETF (IAU) that holds physical gold and tracks its price the way GLD does, but it holds only 86 tonnes. We will be discussing the relative benefits and disadvantages of the most popular ETFs in the products section of the book.

These funds have a massive cumulative effect on the gold market. As demand from individual and institutional investors continues to rise, they will buy gold and issue more shares. That buying increases aggregate demand and probably has contributed to the rise in gold prices over the last five years. More investors are still choosing to hold physical gold bullion, but bullion ETFs are gaining in popularity because they provide easy, liquid, low-cost access to the asset that may be superior to holding bullion physically, depending on one's personal risk tolerance. Although gold prices are certain to rise and fall over time, this buying pressure from large groups of investors that had limited access to gold investments 20 years ago will provide long-term underlying bullish pressure on the market. This is one of several reasons we are forecasting that gold is just at the beginning of a long-term upward trend. As more small and medium-size investors realize that a gold component in their portfolios is necessary for them to be properly diversified, gold ETFs and funds should continue to grow.

BULLION BANKS

So far we have kept the discussion about how the gold market works somewhat simplified. The market has major sellers and buyers who are active right now, and we know that there are some major sellers and buyers that probably will become more active in the future. If everything stayed that way, it would be very simple to think about the market in terms of supply and demand for a fixed amount of gold that is added to annually through new production. Therefore, if currency fluctuations were mild and gold demand were greater than new supplies, we would assume that prices would rise.

There are a few complexities that we have skimmed over in this explanation because they probably don't matter much to individual investors and won't help them forecast prices more accurately. Unfortunately, there is one complication we can't ignore: the so-called bullion banks. The market gets pretty weird when they are involved and it is in their best interest to keep their activities as opaque as possible, and so they can be pretty tricky to understand. The major central banks have very close relationships with these private firms, as does the IMF, and as the clearing members of the London Bullion Market, most of the world's gold investments flow through their hands at some point.

Any list of bullion banks includes Barclay's Capital (United Kingdom), Deutsche Bank AG London (Germany), Société Générale (France), HSBC (Hong Kong/United Kingdom), Goldman Sachs (United States), JPMorgan Chase Bank (United States), Royal Bank of Canada (Canada), the Bank of Nova Scotia (Canada), and UBS AG (Switzerland). These firms are market makers on the London Bullion Market and are responsible for gold "fixing" (it's not what you think) for large gold transactions. As you can imagine, these banks are full of smart, confident financial innovators who are not shy about risk. The bullion banks provide liquidity in the market, and one of the ways they do that as a market maker is through leverage and lots of it. An ugly secret about gold (the ultimate safe-haven investment) is that it is also highly leveraged, but we don't know for sure how leveraged it is. Because of leverage gold supplies are double counted, but they aren't usually disclosed that way.

Here is how it works: Imagine that a bullion bank wants to sell 50 tonnes of gold on the market and the French government is willing to lend the bank the gold with which to do it. This isn't an unusual trade in the financial markets; it's basically what you are doing when you short a stock. The central bank will be paid interest on the gold it has lent, and the bullion bank anticipates making money on the trade. It's a real win-win scenario, right? The problem arises when you try to figure out how global gold supplies have been affected by the trade. The French government isn't going to disclose that it has lent it out, so its balance stays the same and the new buyer is also counted. All of the sudden we have 100 tonnes of gold in the market where we used to have only 50 tonnes.

Now imagine that this transaction takes place thousands of times. How many gold supplies have now been double counted? We don't know, and the spectrum of estimates ranges from the completely insane to the merely alarming. Currently the Federal Reserve is under pressure to increase its transparency through more disclosure, including its transactions with the major bullion banks. This is probably a good thing, and one hopes the trend toward more transparency will continue so that we can all see what the leverage is really like in the gold market. We want to know because investors are concerned that the central banks could be lending too much to the bullion banks to keep gold prices low and currency values high, which in turn keeps interest rates low. Central banks intervene in asset markets all the time to prop up prices and achieve their own strategic objectives, and so it is not a stretch to assume they are doing the same thing in the gold market. Quantitative easing is just one example of a strategy the Fed is using to keep interest rates low and Treasury debt prices high, so why wouldn't it be doing the same thing in the gold market? Unfortunately, the magnitude of this issue isn't known right now, so we wait.

Until we have more transparency in the gold bullion market, we won't know what is being lent to the bullion banks and what the terms of those loans are, but the bright side of all this is that most traders assume that if we did know what was going on, it would mean that gold is undervalued, not overvalued. We tend to believe that this uncertainty is already priced into the market, but if there is still a major disconnect between reported supplies and actual supplies, it is likely to be good for gold prices. The dark side of this uncertainty is that the problems lurking in the shadows could be major enough to cause big economic disruptions. The credit default swap (CDS) and subprime mortgage financing markets nearly brought Western economies to a full collapse in 2007–2008, and so it isn't a stretch to assume that the leverage used in the gold market could be disruptive in a bad way as well.

INDIVIDUALS

A little less than half the aggregate demand for gold each year is for jewelry. As you can imagine, when the global economy is booming, demand for gold as a discretionary consumer product rises and this can drive the price of gold higher. However, this kind of distributed demand is very difficult to measure, and trends are tough to identify. Individual or "retail" investors also buy gold deposits at a bank or invest in bars and coins. Retail investors are surprisingly active and were on track to absorb almost 1,000 tonnes of gold by the end of 2010. Demand was already strong in the retail sector as the credit crisis began to take off in 2007, and we expect that this is a trend that will continue in the near term. Continued quantitative easing, tight markets, and deficit spending will provide motivation for retail investors to seek asset protection through physical gold holdings. We will be discussing the investment alternatives available in the physical gold market in the products section of the book. Holding gold is actually quite expensive and can be difficult for small or inexperienced investors compared with ETFs or gold futures, but popularity and demand are stimulating innovation and we expect that better choices will continue to emerge.

GOLD PRODUCERS

Gold producers also play a major role in the market and we will discuss gold companies as an investment opportunity a little later in the book, but for now the role that these companies play as the supplier of new stores of gold should be obvious. If prices are high, mining production can be expanded or maintained, which should have some influence on supply in the market. Gold producers have been relatively stable over the last few years, and their influence on prices mostly has been positive since the industry changed its hedging practices in the early 2000s.

When the central banks in Europe agreed to throttle sales of gold on an annual basis in 1999, the largest gold producers in the world began changing the way they were hedging future prices. A side benefit of the change was that market participants can be more confident about higher prices in the future. The way producers used to hedge against future prices was essentially the same as accelerating supply. When they stopped hedging, supply was taken out of the market, which is good for gold prices. Why gold producers have reduced their hedging practices is a little complicated and beyond the scope of this book, but the bottom line is that the negative impact producers used to have on the market has been reduced. Most traders assume that producers will continue operating this way (without large hedges), but if that situation changed, it would be telegraphed to the market very quickly because so many of these firms are public and are required to make disclosures.

CHAPTER 3

The Fundamentals of the Gold Market

Fundamental analysis is something that traders usually associate with the stock market rather than with gold and other currencies. Whereas fundamental analysts in the stock market look at the financial statements for a specific firm, gold analysts monitor macroeconomic factors, political stability, and competition from investment alternatives to forecast prices. Analysis like this is not a science, and because you are using current data to predict the future, you have to assume that fundamental models will not be very accurate. This is true for any analytical methodology, and the accuracy problem isn't a bad thing; it's just a reality we have to live with as investors.

There is a long list of gold fundamentals we could detail in this section; however, it has been our experience that you get sharply diminishing returns from adding more indicators and analyses. Keep in mind that no matter what we know about why gold supposedly moved yesterday or today, we are using fundamental analysis to predict the future, and so there is only so much we can do to improve accuracy. This is actually good news because it means there is less work to do before making a trading decision. Because of gold's role as an alternative currency and safe-haven investment, we suggest that almost all the fundamental factors that have a meaningful impact on the forces of supply and demand can be summarized in one underlying issue: investor fear. By "investor" we mean the major players as well as the small individual traders (they are more alike than you might assume), and by "fear" we mean the level of confidence (or lack of confidence) about economic growth, political stability, government solvency, and monetary disruptions.

Because gold does not offer yields to investors the way a bond or stock does, its role is mostly that of a safe-haven investment or a hedge against extreme risks. Hedges don't perform well when confidence is high, but because gold acts like insurance against major unknowns, it tends to do very well when fear becomes extreme. The financial crisis of 2007–2011 is a classic example of this kind of market environment. Gold was already in a bull market as U.S. dollar weakness and an emerging subprime mortgage crisis in mid-2007 began to accelerate the rise in gold prices. The rally continued to gain momentum as the real estate and mortgage crisis in the United States began spreading like a virus around the world. Financial markets were in danger, and some even collapsed. That level of uncertainty is overwhelming, and gold began to appreciate at a much faster rate despite the fact that inflation (another fundamental factor for gold) in the United States was relatively low.

During the current period the big issues the world's financial markets have been grappling with are so severe that investors have no historical precedents or experience to fall back on to guide their future actions. This level of uncertainty is crippling in some markets but can be very good for gold prices. This is especially true when fear is centered in or comes from the world's major economies, such as the United States, Europe, China, and Japan. Gold prices will not respond this way to similar issues that occur on a smaller scale in emerging markets or even in small established economies. Because gold is an asset that responds strongly to fear, it is also subject to bubbles and fast corrections. When the factors causing the original uncertainty begin to resolve and growth resumes, gold can enter unexpected bear markets. From a gold bull's perspective, rising confidence levels are a bad thing. This is one of several reasons why we will spend time in this book talking about what you can do to protect yourself from a bursting bubble in the gold market.

A classic example of this cycle of confidence and fear and how it affects the gold market can be seen in the events leading up to the stock market crash of October 1987 and the subsequent collapse of the gold bubble in 1988 and 1989. The crash of October 1987 remains the largest and fastest decline in percentage terms in U.S. stock market history, but it is important to realize that even before the crash uncertainty and fear were on the rise. Inflation in the United States and Europe had been growing during the years before the crash, and in response the United States began raising rates very quickly. A cross-Atlantic argument with Germany about the appropriate use of monetary policy to solve the problem emerged because the United States' actions were making the situation worse in Europe. Does this sound familiar? It should because similar issues are occurring now between the United States, Europe, and China. When the world's largest economies begin arguing in public about monetary policy, investors get scared. Eventually, rising rates and a stronger U.S. dollar led to a very sharp correction in the bond markets of the United States and Europe in early 1987, and the disruption spread like a virus.

Eventually that fear bled into the stock market, and the October 1987 crash occurred. However, before that time fear already had driven gold prices up more than 60 percent. The crash turned out to be short-lived, with the stock market closing up by the end of 1987 (barely). The major economic factors that created the fear and the crash began to fade very quickly, and the stock market continued its rally by setting new highs in July 1989. The good news is that gold investors enjoyed a long bull market that would have offered significant diversification benefits during the

1987 crash, but caution was needed because gold topped out by the end of 1987 and it took less than 18 months for bullion prices to decline 30 percent. The run-up in gold prices before the actual crash is another great example of gold acting as a leading indicator before a big move in stocks. However, many traders delayed their purchases of gold until the crash and were buying at the high when the news looked worst. It took another 18 years for gold to get back to 1987 levels when confidence in the U.S. economy began to erode again. Two years later, when "froth" began to appear in the sub-prime mortgage market, gold finally beat the inflation-adjusted prices of 1987 and long-term gold investors started to make profits.

The 1987 crash is legendary, and until 2008 it was the most recent benchmark for major market disruptions. There are a lot of lessons to be learned from that period of history, but perhaps the most important is the effect fear and confidence can have on gold prices. Gold tends to run up when investors feel the need for a hedge but before the assets they are really worried about have collapsed. As a leading indicator, gold's relationship with fear can be very effective. As we walk through the fundamentals of the gold market, look for the common denominators of investor fear and confidence. You will find that asking the question "Will this issue worsen fear or increase confidence?" provides the necessary context for understanding how and why gold is sensitive to economic fundamentals.

Before we dig into the factors that contribute to investor fear and confidence, we should discuss a trap hidden in this kind of analysis that can trip up many traders. When we talk about investor fear, we don't mean your fear. You are not the market any more than we are, and what we think about gold, inflation, or monetary policy has no ability to influence prices whatsoever. If you are very fearful of a currency collapse but the market isn't, you will lose. It doesn't matter what your political feelings are or how thorough you think your analysis is; if the market disagrees with you, it won't do you any good. This sounds like a strange comment to make, but it is absolutely critical to understand that there is a difference between what you think should happen and what actually happens in the market. Proper diversification and being somewhat skeptical about your own analysis are the two best ways to increase your odds of profiting from the gold market in the long term.

THE FIVE FUNDAMENTAL FACTORS

Without further ado here are the five fundamental factors we think affect investor fear and therefore gold prices the most.

Inflation

Inflation does affect the price of gold, but not as reliably as you might assume. Many new gold investors believe that if there is inflation in the United States, gold should be rising in value because it will cost more inflated dollars to buy an ounce. However, over the long term there isn't a very strong correlation between inflation and gold prices. We believe that there are two fundamental reasons for this. First, gold is not a commodity that is consumed like oil or steel, and so it responds to purchasing power differently than do other commodities; second, gold must compete for yields when an economy is growing, which is often when inflation is at its highest.

What actually causes inflation is debated and there are a number of different factors at play, but we can assume that much of it is due to growth in the money supply. That was true under gold standards and is definitely a factor under the current global system of fiat, or unbacked, currencies. Most central banks subscribe to the theory that a moderate level of inflation is beneficial for an economy because it motivates investment and relieves debt burdens over time. Therefore, it is "normal" to see monetary supply and inflation grow over time. Figure 3-1 shows the consumer price index (CPI) graphed against gold prices over the last 30 years. The inflation

FIGURE 3-1

Spot gold prices versus consumer price index, January 1980–December 2010.

Source: World Gold Council/Federal Reserve Bank of St. Louis

trend is relatively smooth, which is what we would expect if the Federal Reserve was intentionally trying to hit an annual minimum inflation target; however, as you can see, there isn't a very strong correlation between gold and consumer prices, whereas there is between gold and currency values; this is something we discussed previously.

Inflation and growth often occur together, and as long as inflation doesn't lead to fear, gold is likely to remain flat. In a situation like that, gold investors may get stuck in a value trap. Higher yields in stocks, bonds, and commodities attract capital, and demand for gold can remain very soft. Conversely, gold sometimes rallies during periods of disinflation (declining rates of inflation) such as 2008–2010; this may seem counterintuitive, but this inverse correlation between gold and inflation can last for extended periods.

It is important to differentiate between "normal" levels of inflation and very high levels of inflation or even hyperinflation. You can assume that if inflation exceeds normal levels and fear begins to rise, gold prices will act as expected and begin to climb as well. In the late 1970s and early 1980s the United States experienced extreme rates of inflation without growth, and gold prices subsequently hit all-time highs against the dollar. In fact, if you adjust the price of gold since the high in early 1980 to account for inflation, it has never been as high as it was during that period. That should tell you something about what extreme fear and excessive inflation can do to the price of gold.

The underlying factor that makes the difference between the kind of inflation that doesn't trigger a rise in the price of gold and the kind of inflation that does is investor confidence. If inflation is occurring during a period of growth, confidence is also likely to be very high, and that will make gold a relatively unattractive investment; however, if inflation is very high during an environment of low confidence and high levels of fear, you should expect gold prices to increase very quickly. That is closer to the kind of market environment many gold analysts (including the authors) are projecting over the next few years. The bottom line is that inflation is a factor in gold prices, but not just any kind of inflation will do. If gold must compete with higher yields in a moderately inflationary environment, it isn't likely to do very well. However, if inflation is excessively high or is expected to be very high in the near term and growth is low, it will amplify returns and gold investors will see large profits.

Currency Fluctuations

We intentionally put currency exchange rate fluctuations after inflation in this list of key fundamentals because although they are two different things, they are often confused with each other. On a daily basis we speak to a large U.S. and international audience via the Internet or in person, and we get questions all the time from viewers who confuse a falling currency in the international market with an inflating currency. Currency fluctuations describe the relationship that one currency, such as the U.S. dollar, has with other global currencies or a basket of global currencies. If the dollar falls in value versus the yen, it does not mean that the U.S. dollar is inflating, nor does it mean that a weaker currency is a bad thing.

We think that U.S. investors and consumers often misinterpret a weakening U.S. dollar on the international market as a bad thing because of the words we use to describe that movement. Talking about your currency as weak, bearish, or falling carries negative connotations, but in the currency market those negatives don't apply the same way that they might for a stock or bond. For example, mercantile economies (nationalistic economies that depend on a big trade surplus) such as China, Brazil, and Japan would very much like to have a weak currency and actively manipulate the market to make that happen.

Just as a weaker currency on the international market does not mean that inflation is occurring, a strengthening currency in the global market does not mean that the economy is experiencing deflation or disinflation. Because gold is a currency (mostly), exchange rate fluctuations have a reliable impact on the value of gold over the long term. If the dollar is weakening against the other major reserve currencies, it is pretty safe to assume that gold should be rising at the same time. Like the U.S. dollar and the euro, gold is a reserve currency and is sensitive to changes in the forex. This presents a risk for gold investors who are anticipating high global inflation rates over the next few years. If inflation levels outside the United States are greater than those in the United States, we may see a flight into U.S.-denominated assets again, and that will create a stronger dollar, which could inhibit gold prices.

Figure 3-2 shows a good example of what happens to gold when the dollar weakens. The historical context behind this chart was a move in 2000 by the U.S. central bank, under the leadership of Alan Greenspan, to improve liquidity in the United States by lowering interest rates below historical norms. The purpose of that

FIGURE 3-2

Spot gold prices versus U.S. dollar index values, January 2000–December 2010.

Source: Federal Reserve

campaign was to minimize the impact of the emerging recession and maintain full employment, which is the second part of the Federal Reserve's dual mandate. Falling interest rates in the United States and a declining equity market drove the U.S. dollar into a long-term downtrend. The figure shows the U.S. dollar index, which measures the value of the U.S. dollar against a basket of other global currencies. Most of the basket is a mix of the euro, the yen, and the British pound, with the remainder allocated across a smattering of other global currencies. As the dollar declined on low yields (interest rates) in the United States and higher rates internationally, gold also started to rally. You will find that the years 1999–2001 were a profound crossroads in the gold market. Throughout the book we will point out why the events of those three years were so important from a fundamental perspective and how those fundamentals remain unchanged today.

This was a very important bull market for gold prices, and it has fundamentally changed the future of gold. The timing for a gold bull market couldn't have been better. Investors in the United

States had very heavy stock exposure and were being hurt by the bear market that followed the dot-com crash, and at the same time online trading and account management were pushing more investors to take control of their investments and move into gold with a minimum of effort. It had never been like this before, and it helped push much more demand into the market than there would have been otherwise. Gold as an asset is now held by a more diverse pool of investors than ever before, and it continues to gain favor as a legitimate part of a diversified portfolio. We expect that the momentum created by this bull market will continue to drive gold prices for years to come as demand for the asset by small investors continues to grow and more products are created to provide access to the market.

If the dollar continues to weaken against global currencies, we expect that this will have a very positive impact on gold prices. Currently, the U.S. Federal Reserve is in the middle of a concentrated campaign to drive up the supply of dollars to improve credit liquidity and motivate new investment. The amount of money supply that has been created in the United States since 2008 is difficult to compare with that in any other period. As we write this, the Fed is releasing another $600 billion in a second round of so-called quantitative easing that will be added to the trillions of dollars it has deployed since 2007. It is hard to imagine that these actions won't lead to further weakness in the dollar across the international market.

We still need to keep in mind that the United States is not alone in taking extreme measures like this over the last few years. The euro zone is dealing with a serious sovereign debt problem that will require massive expansion in the money supply to avoid defaults, and China has been increasing bank reserves as it struggles to keep a handle on extreme levels of inflation. These disruptions among other emerging problems could lead to a second collapse in the financial markets that could play spoiler for a weak dollar trend as many investors would seek shelter in U.S.

dollar–denominated assets. We expect future disruptions to be temporary, but we should remain flexible just in case.

Global Risk Discounting

After financial market disruptions, war or the threat of war is the most significant source of uncertainty for investors. Because of gold's role as a safe-haven investment, it tends to do well when investors are most fearful, and war would certainly cause such a market condition. War is also closely associated with other factors that will drive up prices, including excess spending, money printing, political instability, and currency crises. This is a sensitive subject, but unfortunately war or the threat of war can have a material impact on your portfolio, and it will require you to take some action.

As we have been writing this book, tensions between North Korea and South Korea have been headline news. On November 23, 2010, North Korean forces shelled a South Korean island, killing four people. This was terrible news for everyone, and Figure 3-3 shows the impact the news had on gold prices. Investors seeking a shelter or safe haven drove up gold prices to new all-time highs (as measured in absolute dollar terms) before debt problems in Europe interrupted the trend. As we write this, all-out war has not broken out on the Korean peninsula, but the market is still very choppy while gold traders wait for resolution one way or the other.

It is not a coincidence that the bottom of the long-term bear market in gold ended toward the end of 2001 after the United States invaded Afghanistan. The rally in gold accelerated dramatically in 2003 once the United States invaded Iraq. In many ways this was a perfect storm for gold investors. Spending associated with a long-term war is extremely dilutive for a currency, and when combined with a low interest rate environment and agreements by the world's major central banks to limit gold sales, it seems inevitable that gold would hit all-time-high prices seven years later. Not all wars or threats have the same impact on the gold market. War directly

FIGURE 3-3

Daily chart of gold spot prices, August 2010–December 2010.

Source: MetaStock

involving the United States, Europe, Japan, and China will have a much larger impact than will war involving smaller economies. A war that is likely to be protracted and lengthy is also likely to have a much larger impact on gold prices. For example, although the first Gulf War contributed to a small spike in gold prices in 1990, its limited scope (compared with the invasions of Afghanistan and Iraq two decades later) led investors to dump gold as a safe-haven investment in the short term.

Interest Rates

We have mentioned that gold is sensitive to interest rates because it is a nonyielding asset; however, that isn't exactly true. Gold can be leased for a return and large gold deposits do collect interest at times, but an individual investor is not likely to have a deposit large enough for the yield to be very meaningful. Individual investors should not expect to earn income from gold investments; for most traders, it will cost money to invest in gold. That means that gold will be very sensitive to alternatives that offer income potential such as bonds or even dividend-bearing stocks. Higher yields in the bond market when the economy is good can have a long-term bearish impact on gold prices unless there is some other mitigating factor.

A good interest rate benchmark to use in your analysis is the yield on the 10-year U.S. Treasury note because it is in the middle of the yield curve, has a strong relationship to housing and the economy, and is extremely liquid. Figure 3-4 shows the yield on this bond compared with gold prices over the period 2008–2010. Although the relationship isn't perfect, you can see a remarkable inverse correlation. When yields are rising, there is a high probability that the trend in gold will flatten or even fall, whereas declining yields tend to result in a very positive move in gold prices. This chart is typical of this relationship on a short-term basis and also can be applied (more or less) over the long term.

Besides competition for yields, this relationship exists because government bonds and very high-grade corporate bonds (especially U.S. Treasury bonds) are also safe-haven investments during times of uncertainty and fear. When traders demand bonds as a store of value, it drives prices up and yields down. When yields on the 10-year Treasury note broke long-term support in November 2008, gold responded very quickly and nearly doubled in price over the subsequent two years. This intermarket relationship between gold and yields can produce very accurate trade triggers for short-term traders as well as entry opportunities for long-term investors. For example, to offset the recession in the early 2000s, the Federal Reserve began driving interest rates very low, which caused longer-term investors to begin moving out of lower-yielding bonds and into gold for diversification. Since that time, 10-year

FIGURE 3-4

Weekly chart of gold spot prices (candlesticks) versus 10-year yield index (solid line), January 2009–December 2010.

Source: MetaStock

Treasury yields have been cut in half and real yields (net of inflation) are very near 0 percent; this has helped contribute to a perfect storm for bullish gold prices in this decade. The Fed has given no indication that it will attempt to drive rates back up in the near term, which means there is a very high likelihood that gold will continue to benefit from an extremely low interest rate environment for at least the next two years.

Keep in mind that yields or interest rates can go up unexpectedly in a low- or negative-growth environment. This is a rare but real possibility over the next few years. In that kind of market gold might not respond as predictably as one would expect. In 1980 these conditions (low growth and high interest rates) actually led to gold's all-time-high price (when adjusted for inflation); however, similar conditions in 1981 and 1982 were accompanied by a massive drop in gold prices. Current market conditions are not the same as those in the period 1980–1983, but it is a good example of how unpredictable gold can get when interest rates rise while growth is flat or negative. If you are interested in doing more research on this unusual relationship, we recommend visiting the Economic Research Tools (FRED—Federal Reserve Economic Data) at the St. Louis Federal Reserve Bank's Web site.

Gold Supply and Demand

The forces of supply and demand in the gold market are a bit of a puzzle. If the major sources of supply in the gold market were more distributed, this wouldn't be as difficult a discussion, but as we have pointed out, the big gold investors, including central banks, the IMF, and major funds, can each have a very concentrated impact on the market. The influence of these major supply sources can at times overwhelm demand for gold jewelry and investment. It is also possible for these big investors to become such a large source of demand that they overwhelm increased production and slack investment interest in the private sector. As a fundamental analyst you will need to make certain assumptions about these investors and what kind of an impact they will have on the market over the next few years. We are forecasting that the big gold traders (like individual traders) are going to need to acquire gold bullion as an asset for diversification purposes and that that should put them on the demand side of the equation, but we will be watching carefully for potential changes.

Most of the demand for gold is split more or less evenly between investment and jewelry. Jewelry used to represent a much larger percentage of demand relative to investment, but over the last few years the two have been approaching parity. The World Gold Council projected that at the end of 2010 annual global demand for gold would be over 3,700 tonnes, of which 1,311 (35 percent) tonnes would be for gold as an investment and approximately 2,000 (54 percent) tonnes would be for jewelry. Demand has continued to be strong in Western economies, with a lot of growth in both India and China. For example, demand for gold jewelry in India in the third quarter of 2010 was 36 percent higher than in the same period the year before and was up over 62 percent for the last 12 months.[1] We expect that trend to continue as long as economic growth in the region remains strong. The story in China and several other emerging market economies is very similar.

As the economic powerhouses of India and China continue to improve, we are forecasting that they will be net gold buyers for investment, reserves, and jewelry. It seems unlikely that the U.S. dollar will emerge from the 2008–2011 rounds of quantitative easing and debt monetization with the same status it had during the 1990s and early 2000s, which would protect gold in those markets from competition as a safe-haven investment. Growth and weakness in the dollar will put longer-term pressure on the demand side of the gold market as a safe-haven investment and currency hedge. Economic growth will create more individual gold buyers for both jewelry and investment. As a side note, increased global growth in developed and emerging markets also should support industrial demand for gold; however, prices are not likely to be as sensitive to changes on that side of the market.

Ultimately, a good gold investor will have to be aware of potential changes on both the demand and supply sides of the gold market. Potential shifts in sentiment in the official and private sectors are not a bad thing because they tend to support long-term trends that can be productive to the upside or the downside. Being successful in the market will partly be a function of an investor's willingness to be flexible and responsive to major shifts in this fundamental factor.

---

[1] World Gold Council, "Gold Demand Trends Q3, 2010."

CHAPTER 4

The Bad and the Worst Gold Products

Before we begin digging into specific gold investing strategies, we want to spend some time on the products that we recommend and those we don't. We will start with the bad products and move up from there. As finance writers and investment managers we get a lot of feedback and correspondence from readers and viewers, and some of the most energetic responses are from investors who defend scams or bad products. We don't know whether this is a case of Stockholm syndrome or wishful thinking, but the sad fact is that there are a lot of scams in the gold market. Some of the products we will throw into this category aren't technically illegal, but they are bad enough to be called scams.

Fortunately, there are also many great products available for investors, making this a great time for short- and long-term investors to diversify into gold. The next two sections will help you understand the differences among the products that are available and explain why one may be preferable to another, depending on one's investing objectives and personal preferences. This list is not comprehensive; what we have tried to do is include enough detail about what makes a product good or bad that you can apply the same tests to other products you may be considering. Always do your own research before buying gold investment products because their risk characteristics, fees, and structure change from time to time and you should know what you are getting into before you integrate an investment into your portfolio.

We should also note that there are a few products that don't fall into any of the three categories we will discuss. Swaps, forwards, gold deposits, and other institutional-level investment products are probably not suitable to individual investors and are not needed to be successful in today's market.

"HEY, BUDDY, WANNA BUY SOME GOLD COINS?"–IDENTIFYING SCAMS

As we mentioned previously, this section will be controversial for some investors. Some of the products mentioned below may not be scams in the sense that they could be criminally prosecuted, but we feel that their marketing and operational practices are so misleading and biased against the individual investor that they fall into a gray area. This is controversial because some investors have a great desire to believe in a scam. To a certain extent we understand that, but sooner or later (preferably sooner) all the victims figure it out.

When the price of gold rises the way it has over the last few years, there is a lot of money to be made as the market heats up. In a growing market many investors begin feeling a sense of urgency that they need to do something but aren't sure how to take action. The feeling of urgency or the fear of a lost opportunity is cultivated by scammers who hope to take advantage of rushed decisions by selling a bad product or stealing your money altogether. The gold market is not unique in this respect, and many of the typical characteristics of gold investing scams apply to investment scams in general. There are just too many scams in the gold market to mention each version individually, and so we will limit our discussion to two topics: (1) the most common types of scams and (2) the characteristics that almost all investing scams share. This is some-

thing we have written about many times, and we are very passionate about the topic because scammers tend to target those individuals least able to tell the difference or defend themselves.

Advance Fee Frauds

Most traders will recognize this as a so-called Nigerian 419 scam.
However, there are many versions of this fraud that are a lot more
sophisticated than the spam we have all seen in our e-mail in-
boxes. Most often this scam entails an offer to participate in the sale
of a very large amount of gold, and all the scammer needs from
you is a small accommodation fee and/or a United States–based
bank account. We were a little surprised when a scam like this
appeared in the mail at our office recently while we were working
on the book. The scam was obvious, but the quality of the paper,
the envelope, and the language was surprisingly high. We suspect
that the scammers bought a list of individuals in the United States
who receive investment magazines or newsletters (the authors
would definitely qualify) and then sent a bulk mailer to see if they
could catch anyone in their net. Our goal is to make sure you recognize these kinds of gold scams even when they don't appear in
your e-mail in-box.

A reader sent us a note after we ran an article about this gold
scam that was simply amazing. She had received a letter from a
"long-lost relative" who was serving in the U.S. armed forces in
Iraq. Apparently, this person was staying in a home that had
belonged to a prominent member of the deposed Baath party. The
relative had found a cache of gold bullion worth several million
dollars hidden in the home but had no way to get the gold out of
the country without some financial help. The letter was accompanied by pictures of the gold, the "relative," and the surrounding
area. The relative claimed to have been referred by another family
member who wanted to remain nameless. All this was quite compelling, and the addition of the photos was something we hadn't

seen before. Of course, our reader was suspicious and contacted the authorities, who said that this was a version they had been seeing lately and that it was definitely a fraud.

The key characteristic of an advance fee fraud is the advance fee part of the transaction. Big promises are made, but the scammer needs some kind of financial help before the transaction can be completed. That may mean access to your bank account or credit card or a mail-order transfer of some kind. We used a couple of extreme versions of the scam in this section, but advance fee scams are often much more subtle and include things such as autotrading software, access to estate sale lists, and so-called gift networks. Fortunately, the gold market is liquid enough that you can get started as an investor without having to pay more than a small commission up front.

High-Yield Investment Programs

These scams are often called HYIPs and are usually nothing more than pyramid schemes. Essentially, each new recruit "invests" in gold through the program and receives payments that are based on the asset's performance and the number of other "investors" the scammers are able to recruit. Obviously, these scams tend to run out of steam quickly, but not before a lot of money and a lot of friendships have been lost. We have seen several versions of this scam that are marketed as a way to help your friends and family financially, and they are particularly popular in very close social organizations such as religious groups and clubs.

A true pyramid scam usually has a lot of testimonials and relies on personal connections to recruit new capital. These scams obviously are not audited, and it is impossible to inspect the assets that the organization supposedly owns. The gold pyramid scams that we have seen blow up usually never had any gold at all—only promises. We always suggest that before investing in a gold fund or investment one do some due diligence by checking it out with the NFA (National Futures Association), FINRA (Financial Industry Regulatory Authority), or the SEC (Securities and Exchange Commission). We will go into more detail a little later in the book about how to do that for oneself.

Autotrading Programs and Systems

We will discuss autotrading programs and systems again when we cover over-the-counter (OTC) gold dealers and explain why gold investors probably should pass on those firms for now. In addition to the deficiencies we will outline later, OTC dealers are often the tool that autotrading scammers use to perpetrate their theft. The scammers will tell you that if you subscribe your trading account to their autotrading service, they will execute trades automatically within your account. The promised profits can be very exciting but are always fake.

The scam takes advantage of the programmability of the most popular trading software used by large OTC firms. Usually this is MetaTrader, which is a product developed by MetaQuotes, a Russian firm that provides the trading platforms used by most OTC gold dealers. On the surface this functionality is great and can save a lot of time and enable experienced traders to make portfolio adjustments even when they are not available to make a change. Similarly, it is very easy for the scammers to aggressively overtrade your account, generating income for them and losses for you. Because scammers usually are not allowed to have direct access to your accounts, they will have you install a program into the trading application that will execute trades on the basis of "signals" from the scammer's account or trading system. Sometimes, in addition to whatever the scammers are charging for the autotrading service, the OTC dealer will pay the scammers a commission based on the number of trades their victims make. As you can imagine, the incentives are aligned for the scammer to churn your account as frequently as possible, take the commissions, and run.

It seems strange that such a scam could even exist, but similar autotraders operate in the stocks and options market as well. To the novice trader they can be compelling and are often backed up by legitimate-looking account statements, track records, and testimonials. Because what the scammer is doing is technically legal (for reasons that are too complicated to explain here), the victims have no recourse against the scammer or the OTC gold dealer. For the most part these scams are easy to avoid. If you see a pitch for a program or trading system that seems to offer high returns produced by very short-term trading strategies, you can assume that it is an autotrading scam and that those returns will never materialize. In general, if you don't understand exactly why a system will be profitable, you should avoid it. Investing is not that complicated, and so a legitimate strategy should be relatively easy to understand.

Counterfeit Gold

For gold investors the old saying "Don't take any wooden nickels" could be rephrased as "Don't take any brass coins." Scams like this are simple: The scammer has gold coins, bars, or dust for sale, often at below-market prices. There are a number of pretenses to explain why the seller has such inexpensive gold available, but unfortunately, it is most likely counterfeit gold. Most small investors will not go through an assaying process before making a gold bullion purchase because they are not buying enough to make it worth the cost. Scammers know this and try to make many small deals before taking their money and disappearing. As a general rule, if you are offered the opportunity to buy gold for less than its market price, someone is trying to trick you into buying something that is not what you thought it was.

The scams are often done through the mail, and so there is no way to inspect the product before you buy it. We don't have any objections to investing in physical gold bullion, but there are almost always reputable local dealers you can buy from in person.

At the very least, buying this way will save you shipping costs, and being there in person means you can check out the dealers with other local traders to make sure they are legitimate.

Off-Exchange Gold Companies or Private Mining Interests

In this book we will be talking about buying publicly listed gold producers and mining companies as an alternative or supplement to gold bullion investing. This is a strategy that will fit many investors' risk profiles and interests, but that recommendation does not extend to small private firms (real or fictional) that claim to "hit a big gold strike at any moment." This warning extends to firms that are technically public but are not listed on an exchange. Many investors know these kinds of companies as shells, reverse mergers, pink sheets, or penny stocks. The reporting and oversight processes for these firms are not the same as those for truly public companies.

The pitch for these kinds of investments usually is based on the idea that you are getting in on the ground floor. That is a compelling idea, but unfortunately most firms that fall into this category don't exist on anything but paper, they have no ability to execute, and they may be lying to you. As usual, if it sounds too good to be true, you can be sure that it is. There is no shortage of large, aggressive financing firms ready to back a small mining company that has a legitimate gold source. There is no reason a small firm would need to go through the additional expense and liability of finding small individual investors to back a venture unless the larger investors that usually do that kind of financing know that that firm does not have good prospects. These kinds of firms are usually chasing small individual investors because the big companies have already turned them down, and that should tell you something about how likely it is for them to actually find gold or increase their current production.

Ponzi Schemes

Most investors are familiar with the concept of a Ponzi-style scam, which was the kind of fraud Bernie Madoff used to steal $65 billion from investors before being arrested in 2009. Basically, the pitch is to invest in a gold fund because they are promising above-market returns. Those returns may be attributed to the skill of the manager or superior access to the gold market, but behind the scenes the fraudster is probably not making any investments at all. As long as new money is injected into the fund at a faster pace than that at which older investors and the scheme's managers are making withdrawals, the fund can survive.

Inevitably these frauds collapse, but that collapse can take a long time to occur. In Madoff's case the scam probably was started sometime in the mid-1990s and lasted for another 15 years. In our experience this is the second most common kind of fraud perpetrated in the gold market, with the first being off-exchange gold companies. If a Ponzi scheme keeps a low profile and the market remains bullish for an extended period, it may continue operating for a very long time. We are confident that there are many Madoff-style Ponzi schemes operating right now that haven't been found out yet.

THE TELLTALE SIGNS OF A SCAM

Although the list of scams could be much longer than what we have provided, other frauds can be identified by the characteristics that all scams share. We have written about these characteristics many times, and it continues to amaze us how many letters and e-mails we receive from individual investors asking if one investing scam or another could possibly be an exception to the rule. A particular fraud may not have all of the following characteristics but probably will have most, and any one of these issues should be enough to throw up a red flag.

Our theory of why investing scams are so popular is that investors want to believe that the claims and promises are true. Sometimes this desire to believe can be so powerful that the victims defend the scammers even after they have been arrested. There was a case that the SEC reported in 2009 in which the victims of a gold trading Ponzi scheme asked the judge to allow the scammer to keep trading. Apparently, although the victims knew most of the money had been stolen, they remained convinced that he would be able to trade their money back into profitability. That guy must have been some kind of salesman.

Proprietary or Special Skills

We call this one the high priests of the temple pitch, which means that only the scammer has the ability to commune with the spirits of the gold market. The scammer somehow knows what no one else does through inside information or some other proprietary source. These scammers are unable or unwilling to share the specifics of their hidden knowledge, and this can create a feeling of urgency on the part of the victims to hand over their money. This may sound a little jaded, but let's face it, those seeking power or profits have been using this method to get what they want for thousands of years.

Unusually Large and Even Profits

There is a very annoying but unavoidable truth about the financial markets: Risk and reward are positively correlated. If you want even returns month over month and year over year, those returns will be small. In contrast, if you want the potential for big profits, your returns very likely will be uneven and the losses can be quite large among your gains. Most investors understand this and fall somewhere in the middle between holding cash in the bank and betting everything on an out-of-the-money gold call option.

This trade-off is unsatisfactory and can be frustrating because most investors want even returns that are also very large, and if a fraudster promises that that is possible, some will be willing to believe it. Some of the most successful scams in history didn't promise mind-blowing returns; instead, the returns were just large enough to be intriguing and to stand above the crowd without looking obvious. These above-average returns almost always are accompanied by a promise that they will also be unusually even.

That was how Bernie Madoff's fraud worked, and several people made this point about the fraud to the SEC years before he was caught in a bond trading Ponzi scheme. In that case it wasn't the opinion of the whistle-blowers that Madoff was a scam artist; it was a mathematical fact, but not even the SEC wanted to listen (not an uncommon issue). The story behind the most famous of these whistle-blowers—Harry Markopolos—is very interesting, and he has an excellent book about his experiences that we recommend to anyone who wants to learn more about how one of the smartest scammers got away with it for so long.

Limited-Time Offer

A limited-time offer or some other premise for scarcity is a common tactic used by scammers. It helps push investors into making a decision quickly, which is likely to be in the scammer's best interest. Creating a sense of urgency is a tactic that has been used by salespeople and scammers alike for as long as selling (honest or otherwise) has been a profession. We have been monitoring a scam for several years on the Internet that has been offering its auto-trading program to the first 100 buyers since 2004. Either they are not selling very many subscriptions or they are (gasp) lying to create a sense of urgency.

Wall Street Fat Cats

This is the "what 'they' don't want you to know" pitch. There are several popular versions of this scam that promise to show you how Wall Street investors such as Warren Buffett, George Soros, and Bill Gates make so much money. A couple of years ago there was a very popular scam about how notable people such as Bill Clinton and Michael Bloomberg got rich investing in gold coins that also fell into this category. According to this particular scam, the biggest investors on Wall Street were making a fortune by investing in gold coins and taking advantage of a mysterious tax loophole to avoid paying taxes on their gains. You could find out how to do it yourself for a small fee.

For the most part these stories are complete fiction. One of the great things about the financial markets is that although it isn't complete, there is a lot of transparency. With a little work and research you can figure out what the professionals know. In any case, it would not be in the best interests of large fund managers to withhold information from investors they could be inviting to participate in their funds for larger management fees.

This list of scam characteristics isn't very long, but we have found that they are quite consistent. Sadly, there are many legitimate companies offering investment products that have these characteristics in some of their marketing materials. If you do a little digging into these "legit" products, you will find that they contain serious problems and are arguably a scam called by a different name. We will be discussing a few of these products next.

BAD OR IMMATURE PRODUCTS

An inevitable side effect of all the great financial innovations in the gold market is the products that probably should not have been developed in the first place. Sometimes the flaws can be tough to spot because the underlying strategy is good but the execution is poor. We have no doubt that a continued bull gold market will place pressure on the competitive environment to improve and solve some of these issues, but in the meantime these products are better avoided.

There are also a few products we have included in this category that have disadvantages that can be minimized if one is careful. For example, gold coins are difficult to store, are expensive to buy or sell, and can be challenging for new investors to understand, but there are some traders who are really passionate about holding them. This product can be improved as long as you are aware of the issues and are willing to take steps to minimize some of the security risks and liquidity problems. We will go into more detail about those issues in this section.

Some of the products we have included in this section are very popular and appear legitimate on the surface, and so we urge you to keep an open mind and do your own research before being tempted to disregard the dangers. In almost all cases, there are great alternatives to these bad products that don't have the same problems, and as the market grows, we expect that more improvements will be made in the future.

Gold Coins

A discussion about the benefits and disadvantages of gold coins is going to be somewhat controversial. There are many gold investors who swear by them, and in theory we agree that gold coins have the potential to be an easy, interesting, and relatively liquid way to make a long-term investment in physical gold bullion. However, there are some major flaws in the gold coin market that can make things very difficult for small investors who don't know the difference between the intrinsic (gold) value and extrinsic (numismatic) value of collectible coins.

Gold coins are a popular way for long-term investors to acquire and hold gold bullion because coins can be fairly uniform and easy to acquire. This is not the most common way to invest in physical gold (bars are more popular by volume), but new investors often start with gold coins because they are marketed heavily on television, magazines, and the Internet. Investing in gold coins can be fun if you have an interest in coin collecting, and that may offset some of the inherent disadvantages, depending on your personal preferences. Gold coins usually are sold for a large premium over the actual value of their gold content. They are not as liquid as actual bullion, and selling them back to the dealer you purchased them from may be impossible or will involve a discount on the price. Part of the problem with coins as an investment and the reason the markup is often very large is that there are two components to their value: the gold content (which varies) of the coin and the numismatic (collectible) value.

We would never recommend gold coins as a way to invest in gold bullion if your primary objective is to have exposure to gold prices. There are much better alternatives if you want to be able to have the actual bullion in your physical possession. Unless you are very interested in coin collecting, this is one of the most expensive and inefficient ways to buy bullion. The Goldline scandal in 2010 was a good example of why it is so difficult to buy gold coins as an investment without coming out on the wrong side of the deal. Goldline is a gold dealer that advertises very actively on the Internet and cable television. You can call Goldline to buy coins and bars, and the call center will try to "upsell" you into larger orders. The *Los Angeles Times* has estimated that Goldline's revenues are almost $1 billion per year. The problem with Goldline that led to congressional hearings was that it was selling those coins with an average markup of 90 percent over the value of their gold content.

Unfortunately, the media became completely distracted by the so-called hard sell techniques used by the Goldline sales staff and a connection to the Fox News commentator Glenn Beck, who was a spokesperson for the company, to focus on the real issue with buying coins from Goldline and similar mail-order gold coin dealers. Markups on coins are standard, and large markups for very rare and collectible coins aren't unusual. The real problem is that a gold coin's value has too many factors for new investors to grasp the first time they buy. A coin has gold value, collectible value, and in many cases a face value that is still negotiable as currency. Some coins are worth a 90 percent markup above their melt value and some aren't, but could you tell the difference? We can't either, and as investors we aren't interested in coin collecting.

The vast majority of gold coins being marketed in magazines, on the Internet, and on television probably have very little collectible value. They are not rare, and investors should expect to pay very little above the value of their gold content. We conducted a survey of reputable gold coin sellers online and in the local area and found that a recently minted American Eagle gold coin (not collectible) was selling at an average markup of 5 percent, which is much more reasonable if what you really want is a gold investment rather than a coin collection. Unfortunately, shipping added another 1 to 2 percent to the markup, but this is still considerably lower than the markup added by less reputable dealers.

Coin dealers aren't supposed to market coins as an investment because they are not registered as securities dealers. However, they can make certain claims about the coins as a collectible that would imply that a buyer is likely to make a profit in the future, so before you decide to buy a collectible, consider the following questions: Do you understand coin condition grades and the effect they can have on a coin's price? Can you safely store a coin and protect its present condition? How confident are you that the coin is in the condition claimed by the Internet, magazine, or television commercial? Until you feel that you can answer these questions confidently, we suggest staying away from the coin market entirely or sticking to newly minted coins offered by reputable dealers. We will go into more detail about getting a good deal on gold coins and bars in the next section.

The situation is even worse for investors who are purchasing privately minted coins. Not only is there a large markup for those coins, they have an important liquidity problem. Assume that you purchased a privately minted coin and then want to sell it when the market changes or you need the access to capital. If that mint won't buy the coin back, which most won't, you will need to sell it elsewhere for its intrinsic gold value only. That means that not only are you losing the markup, you will have to pay for the coin to be assayed (the process of determining the purity of the metallic content of the coin). That process drives up costs, takes a long time, and compounds the problems that began when the coin was purchased.

This is not an argument against investing in physical gold. In fact, there are several great ways to do that, but we tend to favor holding gold with a company that will store, insure, and catalog it for you rather than having it shipped through the mail. We will go into more detail in the next section about some of these alternatives and include a few tips you can use to make sure you are getting the best deal possible.

OTC or Spot Gold Dealers

In the forex market it is very common for an individual investor to use an OTC dealer and software trading platform to speculate on currency exchange rates. Because gold is an unofficial currency, this was an obvious product for these dealers to begin offering. Traders are attracted to OTC dealers because they usually offer access to extreme leverage (100:1 or more), fast execution, commission-free trading, and low account minimums, which can all be very tempting for a small gold trader. However, be careful because the odds are stacked against you in this market.

When you make a trade with an OTC gold dealer, you are making a bet that gold will rise or fall in value but you never take procession of any physical gold. These trades are very similar to a futures contract, but they are not listed on an exchange; instead, they roll over every three days, and the dealer (or a bank) is the counterparty on each position. Trade sizes are described in "lots" that represent 100 ounces of gold, which means that if gold is trading for $1,300 an ounce, a single lot has a nominal value of $130,000. If you had to pay the full $130,000 up front to control those 100 ounces and the price moved from $1,300 an ounce to $1,320, you would have profited $2,000 in that trade because the 100 ounces are now worth $132,000. That is a tidy profit of 1.5 percent if you exit the trade at that time.

That doesn't sound too bad, but what happens if you apply a little leverage? A dealer usually will offer at least a 2 percent margin, or 50:1 leverage, which means that rather than having to put up $130,000 to control 100 ounces, you will have to post only $2,600, or 2 percent of the total, in a margin deposit. If gold prices rise to $1,320 an ounce, you will still have made $2,000 in profits but would have had to tie up only $2,600 to do it. That has turned a moderate 1.5 percent gain into an amazing 76 percent gain. That scenario is attractive and is usually where the marketing stops, but there is another side to this equation. What happens if you post the $2,600 margin requirement to buy a full lot and gold moves down by $20 instead of up? The answer is obvious: It will be catastrophic to a small trader. Losses that can accrue this quickly are difficult to deal with emotionally, and an emotional trader is not a good trader. You can easily become your own worst enemy.

OTC gold usually is traded on a very short-term basis by individuals who aspire to be successful day traders, and although OTC gold dealers don't usually charge commissions, they will make money from traders through the bid-ask spread and slippage. It is the nature of this industry to be pretty closed about how much its clients make or lose on gold contracts; however, there are some data available from the National Futures Association that indicate that more than 90 percent of traders using an OTC gold or forex dealer lose their entire accounts within 24 months. That is not a very promising statistic. OTC dealers are also not very transparent about pricing and order flow because you are trading against the firm as the counterparty instead of against other traders. They create the prices that are shown, and they may create artificial slippage so that they can grab traders that are close to stop-losses or avoid large limit order levels. Recently the CFTC (Commodity Futures Trading Commission, the U.S. futures regulatory agency) and the NFA (National Futures Association, the futures industry standards and licensing association) have been cracking down on these dealers, but the transition has not been smooth. The practice of moving prices to stop out traders, fill market orders at adverse prices, or skip limit orders is often referred to generically as stop hunting and is still a common practice in the industry.

Some OTC dealers claim that they can avoid these issues through a no-dealing-desk (NDD) trading account. According to the marketing, this means that your order either flows through to the prime dealers that provide the liquidity for the OTC firm or will be filled on an electronic communications network (ECN) where it is matched with other orders. Both of these options can help a little, but the big issues of costs and transparency (or their lack) still exist. We feel that the NDD option is not enough of a solution to justify trading gold with a dealer when so many other transparent alternatives exist.

These dealers have an incentive to work against you because they profit regardless of whether each individual trade is losing or gaining. In the case of a gold contract, the dealer usually will collect $0.30 to $0.50 per ounce in the bid-ask spread each time a trade is made. In the industry the average trader will trade 2,000 ounces, or 20 full lots, per month. Those traders may break even, make a profit, or lose, but the dealer still walks away with $600 to $800 in profits from those trades. The dealers take very little risk because they can hedge your trade against other investors who are taking an opposite position or with their prime dealers. Even if the OTC firm has to offset some of its risk with a larger firm or bank (known as a prime dealer), it will be able to do so at a much cheaper spread, keeping its "trade" in the black. The question we always ask individual traders who choose to get involved with an OTC gold dealer like this is how they plan to overcome that slow leak from their accounts.

The real issue here is a lack of accountability. These firms have a lot of value they could offer, but because they are trading against you, there are just too many incentives to act against your interests. Historically, these OTC dealers, or "bucket shops," have been largely unregulated in the United States, but they are coming under more scrutiny and we expect they will begin to improve their trading and business practices in the near term. However, one hazard of this crackdown on the regulatory side is that many traders (who don't understand how the odds are stacked against them) misinterpret the new regulations as an attempt to stop them from being profitable traders. This has driven some investors to close their accounts and reopen them with smaller dealers that have moved overseas to escape regulation. It should send up red flags when a firm intentionally moves to the financial Wild West of Cyprus, Bermuda, China, or Russia to escape U.S. regulations.

Although OTC dealers don't charge commissions, they do have fees, one of which is a daily "rollover" charge on both sides of the transaction, which means that whether you buy or sell a gold lot with a dealer, you will be charged to hold that position every day. If you are short a gold lot, you may be charged a much larger daily fee at rollover because of the interest expense of holding a short gold position. Because this fee usually is charged at a set time each day, it motivates traders to jump out of their trades before the rollover cutoff, which creates another spread for the dealers, and so they make money either way. There are also annual fees, inactivity fees, statement fees, check fees, and other expenses that can add up, depending on how you manage your account.

Believe it or not, there are some redeeming characteristics in the OTC market that we believe will save the industry and allow it to begin attracting good traders. First, the OTC model allows a dealer to offer very flexible contract sizes to new traders. We used the example of contracts that are worth 100 ounces in this chapter, but OTC dealers offer trade sizes that are one-tenth that size called mini-lots or even one-hundredth lot sizes called micros. Some dealers allow their traders to create just about any fraction of a lot size they need, which provides a lot of flexibility for a trader who is concentrating on consistent position sizing.

The technology that has been developed within this industry has been very impressive. Because gold lots are consistent from one dealer to another, they often compete on the basis of technology and tools. These standard-setting technologies offered by OTC dealers include advanced account management, flexible charting, complex order entry, programmable systems and indicators, and point-and-click execution. We hope this technology will jump the gap into the stocks and options world as well. Over the last 10 years we have seen the industry mature a lot, and although there are still serious problems, competitive pressure and a more educated account base eventually will drive it into more legitimate marketing and operations practices. It will be interesting to watch the initial public offerings (IPOs) that are planned by some of the largest OTC dealers in 2011 and the impact that increased transparency will have on the market.

Spread Betting

Spread betting isn't a product that is seen very much in the United States, but it is very popular in the United Kingdom, Asia, and Europe. The concept is pretty much what it sounds like. The investor makes a wager on the price of gold, and if gold goes up, the investor is paid on the basis of how far the market moved. The investor can lose money if gold prices drop. A spread bet isn't like a bet you make in a casino because your risk isn't fixed. Spread betting is similar in a lot of ways to the kind of trading that is done through an OTC gold dealer.

Unlike a bet you place at a casino, a spread bet does not have fixed odds. You may win an unlimited amount assuming that you (or the firm) don't close your trade, and you could lose the entire value of your account if prices move against you unexpectedly. In fact, it is possible, depending on the account agreement, to lose more money than you originally invested. Like the OTC market, spread betting firms offer complex order entry and flexible position sizing, but the fees are higher and the spread (distance between the buy and sell prices) tends to be wider.

Spread betting has its origins in a loophole in the United Kingdom's tax code. Technically, the profits from a spread bet are not subject to capital gains tax, and that has given the industry an indirect subsidy. They quickly began to spread (no pun intended) their marketing message around the globe, and growth has been exponential outside the United States. A version of spread betting known as CFDs (contracts for difference) is also becoming very popular with very short-term novice gold traders. Spread bets, CFDs, and the OTC market all look and act very similarly, and the differences (and disadvantages) are probably inconsequential to the small trader.

The problems of spread betting, CFDs, and the OTC market are identical. There is no transparency, costs are higher than traders think, and it is in the firm's best interest to motivate you to trade (make bets) as often as possible. This means that most, if not all, traders have a negative equity curve. However, some traders enjoy the action and insist that it's no different from playing online poker. For our purposes, we will stick with a strong recommendation to stay away from any firm that acts as the counterparty and charges fees if you don't trade frequently enough.

We always bristle when nontraders refer to investing as gambling; however, depending on the product, they may be right.

Leveraged ETFs

We are huge fans of indexed ETFs because they are cost-efficient, easy to trade, and liquid and offer access to asset classes (such as gold) to small investors in ways that would not have been possible as recently as five years ago. However, indexed ETFs have two evil twins called leveraged and inverse ETFs that have serious problems that are very hard to understand if you are just looking at them on the surface. The primary issue with these funds is that they are designed to match daily returns of gold or gold futures rather than long-term performance. Because they must make frequent adjustments to their assets to match daily performance, these ETFs also carry very high costs.

It is easier to explain why these ETFs are so bad if we compare their performance over different time periods. For this example, we will compare the SPDR Gold Trust ETF (GLD), which is not leveraged and should track actual gold prices quite closely, with the ProShares Ultra Gold 2X (UGL) leveraged ETF, which should go up or down twice as much as GLD does on a daily basis. For the first part of our comparison, imagine that you purchased GLD shares on January 4, 2010, for $109.82 per share. It's a rough estimate, but you usually can assume that one share of GLD is equal to one-tenth of an ounce of gold. Now assume that you sold those shares on October 31, 2010, at the close price of $132.60 for a net gain of 21 percent, which is almost exactly how much the spot price for gold increased over that period.

UGL is leveraged 200 percent, which means that it is designed to move 200 percent the amount of gold prices on a daily basis. On the basis of this information alone, a trader might reasonably assume that UGL should be up 42 percent over the same period. Unfortunately for investors who actually held that position, it is up only 38 percent overall. This underperformance is a big issue and can get worse if the market trends flat or down for an extended period. For example, if we look at the period of May through July 2010, GLD was flat while UGL lost 1.32 percent. During the recent but brief bear market for gold from December 2009 through February 2010, GLD lost 6.76 percent while UGL more than doubled that with a loss of 14.58 percent. The bottom line from these examples is that a 200 percent leveraged ETF is very likely to fall short of doubling the returns of an unleveraged ETF during good times, lose money during a flat trend, and more than double the losses of its unleveraged twin during a downtrend.

This is a problem with all leveraged or inverse ETFs that results from the fact that they are indexed to the daily returns of the asset they are tracking so that they miss out on the benefits of compounding. In the following boxes you can see how this works.

We should note that this example is a little oversimplified. The actual management strategies behind leveraged and inverse ETFs are quite complicated and present risks beyond the compounding problem described above. For example, during periods of falling volatility these funds may perform a little better than expected, but losses can compound very quickly when volatility rises. The bottom line is that the risks and costs of these funds guarantee that you will lose money if you hold the ETF over a long period no matter which direction the market trends. Unless you know in advance that the market will move in an unbroken stream of positive closes,

---

Trading a 200 Percent Leveraged Gold ETF

Day 1. Buy a 200 percent leveraged gold ETF for $100 per share.

Day 2. The market for gold drops 2 percent, which translates to a loss of 4 percent in your stock, which is now worth $96 per share.

Day 3. The market for gold rises 2 percent, or 4 percent for your ETF, which is now worth $99.84 [($96 × 4 percent) + $96 = $99.84 per share].

Day 4. The market really drops, and gold prices plummet 10 percent, which means your stock is now worth $79.87 per share.

Day 5. The market rallies 12 percent, which pushes your stock back up to $99.04 per share. You decide you are done with all this volatility and exit with a 1 percent loss.

Trading an Unleveraged Gold ETF

Day 1. Buy an unleveraged gold ETF for $100 per share.

Day 2. The market for gold drops 2 percent, and your stock is now worth $98 per share.

Day 3. The market for gold rises 2 percent, and your stock is now almost back to breakeven at $99.96 per share.

Day 4. The market really drops, and gold prices plummet 10 percent, which means your stock is now worth $89.96 per share.

Day 5. The market rallies 12 percent, which pushes your stock back up into profitability of $100.75, at which point you decide to take your profits off the table.

---

you are probably much better off looking for another way to use leverage, and in the strategies section of this book we will look at some specific ways to do that.

Inverse ETFs

Eventually, gold prices will correct to the downside, and those bearish trends can be just as productive for an aggressive trader as a bull trend. A savvy investor could certainly short a gold ETF such as GLD to profit from a decline, but that can be a little complicated if you have never done that kind of trade. Inverse ETFs are an attempted solution to this problem, but they have the same compounding problem as leveraged ETFs. Sometimes inverse ETFs are leveraged as well, which makes the problem even more severe. Inverse ETF shares can be purchased like a regular ETF or stock, but they will rise in value if the underlying index or asset they are tracking declines.

To show you why these ETFs are not a good choice for gold bears we will use the same hypothetical prices from the prior example and compare the ProShares UltraShort gold inverse ETF (GLL), which is designed to move 200 percent of the inverse daily price performance in gold prices or GLD. That means that if GLD went down 1 percent on a particular day, GLL should rise 2 percent, or if GLD rose 3 percent on a particular day, GLL should fall 6 percent. Imagine that a bearish trader decided to profit by buying shares in GLL during the brief bear market from December 2009 through February 2010. During that period GLD lost 6.76 percent but GLL profited only 7 percent, which is surprising since the trader in this example would have expected profits closer to 14 percent, or twice the inverse of GLD. This underperformance is caused by the same compounding problem that plagues leveraged ETFs. Inverse ETFs will underperform expectations when the market falls and lose more than you might have expected during a bull market.

To understand why this happens consider the following trade with the same hypothetical daily numbers that were used in the section on leveraged ETFs.

Trading an Inverse and 200 Percent Leveraged Gold ETF

Day 1. Buy an inverse and leveraged gold ETF for $100 per share.

Day 2. The market for gold drops 2 percent, which translates to a gain of 4 percent in your stock, which is now worth $104 per share.

Day 3. The market for gold rises 2 percent, which is a 4 percent loss for your ETF, which is now worth $99.84 ($104 × 96 percent = $99.84 per share).

Day 4. The market really drops, and gold prices plummet 10 percent, which means your stock has rallied and is now worth $119.80 per share.

Day 5. The gold market rallies again, rising 12 percent, which pushes your stock back down to $91.05 ($119.80 × 76 percent = $91.05) per share. The only word for this result is "ouch." Needless to say, you decide to exit the position completely at this point with a 9 percent loss.

Short Trading an Unleveraged Gold ETF

Day 1. Short an unleveraged gold ETF for $100 per share.

Day 2. The market for gold drops 2 percent, and your short is now up $2 because the stock is worth $98 per share.

Day 3. The market for gold rises 2 percent, and your short is still profitable $0.04 with the stock at $99.96 per share.

Day 4. The market really drops, and gold prices plummet 10 percent, which means your short is up over $10 in profits and the stock is priced at $89.96 per share.

Day 5. The market rallies 12 percent, which pushes the stock to $100.75, and your short is now in a small losing position. After all that volatility you are down only 0.75 percent.

The leveraged inverse ETF has lost much more than the outright short position has, and even if we ran the same numbers on an unleveraged inverse ETF, the results would still be surprising, with a loss of more than 5 percent over the same trading period. Once traders discover this weakness, they always ask why these products are still so popular. We have no good answer. At the time of this writing, GLL trades an average of 344,000 shares per day, and every time gold prices get a little choppy for a few days, volume can double or triple the average. Companies that sponsor these ETFs are getting a little better about warning investors about these risks, but the disclaimers are still hard to find.

We have been working with individual investors for a long time, and one of a few things we know for sure is that we all hate reading disclosures and prospectuses, and the vaguer a warning is, the less likely we are to pay attention to it. Litigation about these disclosures is ongoing and eventually will lead to better warnings, but in the meantime it is an important lesson for individual investors to consider before investing in any new gold ETF product. We hope that this section won't be misinterpreted as a warning against shorting gold. Although gold is in a bull market now, it won't be like that forever, and shorter-term traders may want to be able to profit from a temporary decline. Even long-term investors may be interested in being able to profit from a bear market once one begins to emerge. It makes sense for investors to be prepared to profit from the rise in an asset's price as much as from a decline. We will spend time on bearish strategies later in the book.

Futures-Backed ETFs

Gold futures–backed ETFs can be purchased in the same way as the shares of other ETFs, but they represent the performance of a portfolio of gold futures rather than gold bullion. That sounds like a great idea and usually we would suggest that gold futures themselves fall into the good product category, but alas, although futures-backed ETFs are very popular, they are a pretty terrible instrument.

Futures-backed ETFs are more expensive than bullion-backed ETFs, with an average annual management fee of 0.75 percent versus 0.24 to 0.40 percent for the two major bullion-backed ETFs; by itself that isn't terrible, but costs are costs and we should do whatever it takes to minimize them. However, management costs and commissions are not the biggest problem with these ETFs. The real issue is that the fund has to roll over its futures contracts on a nearly monthly basis, and each time it does that, the fund has to pay more to buy the next futures contracts. When a futures contract with a longer expiration date has a higher price than the futures contract that is expiring in the current month, it means the market is in "contango." That small premium being paid each time the fund must roll over its investments adds up quickly. Fund managers claim that this is a disadvantage during a period when the market is in contango, but sometimes futures contracts are actually cheaper for the next month, which is called "backwardation," although you would never hear a real trader use that term. Those periods of backwardation would result in a slight advantage for the fund rolling over gold contracts each month. On the surface this would seem to imply that periods of backwardation offset the intermittent periods of contango, right?

There is only one problem with this theory: Gold is almost always in a state of contango, and there is no reason to assume that this will ever change. It happened briefly in 1999, again in March 2001, and once more in early 2011, but these conditions are extremely rare. We have a hard time picturing the conditions that would produce such a market environment for an extended period. It is upsetting to read the prospectuses of these funds and see this comment being made when everyone with any experience in the market knows that gold is virtually always in contango. The fund companies put it in there to trick traders who don't know better. The damage caused by contango in a futures-backed ETF is not as severe as the compounding issues in leveraged or inverse ETFs, but it is still a big problem, especially for long-term investors. In the beginning of 2007 PowerShares introduced the DB Gold Fund ETF (DGL), which has become a popular futures-backed fund with more than 40,000 shares traded per day. Because of higher costs and contango, the fund has lagged the bullion-backed ETFs such as GLD and IAU by 18 percent since its introduction. That starts to add up for a long-term investor and makes it a product that has some potential but just doesn't have the right execution.

CHAPTER 5

The Good
Gold Products

The products discussed here fall into the good category; however, we would like to be clear that "good" does not automatically equal "suitable." For example, we are big fans of gold futures and gold bullion ETF options because they are extremely liquid and offer very flexible leverage, but we are also willing to be very actively involved in our trading and have a very high tolerance for risk. Not all investors fit that mold, and therefore not all good products should be traded by everyone. Fortunately, there is a large number of investing products for gold traders of all types that are cheap, liquid, transparent, and flexible regardless of one's activity level and risk tolerance. In this section we will discuss some of the best examples from each category and include specific reasons why these products make sense and in what circumstances they should be avoided.

This list of good products is not comprehensive, but it is thorough enough to help you get started on your own investing research. Attempting to provide a complete guide to gold investing products would be futile as the market changes so quickly, but the characteristics of a good product are fairly universal, including low cost, liquidity, efficiency, and flexible use of leverage. Optimizing these factors is important because they are some of the few things we can control as investors. In this section we have included specific tips for maximizing your control over the products you are trading as well as the brokerage where you hold your account.

ETFs

Exchange-traded funds (ETFs) can be traded like a stock and in many ways look like a mutual fund but are superior products in just about every way. We believe that mutual funds are holding on to their market share only because they still have a stranglehold on tax-sheltered investing plans such as 401(k) programs. As the market continues to mature, the balance will keep shifting. ETFs are convenient, liquid, and efficient, but they aren't free. As with any fund, managers have to be paid, and your broker will charge a commission (but not always; more details later). ETFs also carry some special risks if you use them to invest in the gold market, but they are a great tool for diversification and are the lowest-cost way to access the skills of a professional manager and avoid having to do the work yourself.

ETFs solve three very important problems in the mutual fund industry.

Low Costs

Fund managers in the gold market traditionally charged very high fees for their services despite the fact that on average active managers underperform passive indexes. Most gold ETFs are passively managed or indexed, which means that the manager or management team is not attempting to beat the performance of gold or the gold mining industry but only match it. Some indexed ETFs get very close to matching the returns of the index or underlying asset they are following, and overall they tend to get a lot closer than active managers do.

Because an ETF is passively managed, the fees are very low. Depending on the ETF, the costs of investing in gold bullion can be as low as 0.25 percent per year. Compared with actively managed mutual funds, hedge funds, or commodity pools with fees that start at 5 percent the first year, this is a steal. If active managers performed better than passive indexing, we wouldn't be as passionate about gold ETFs, but fortunately for individual investors, they are a superior product.

Tax Issues

Many mutual funds are constructed in such a way that even if the fund loses money, investors may wind up with a tax liability. This can occur when the fund is down overall but the managers sell one or more individual positions within the fund that have been profitable. Taxes have to be paid on those individual profits, which are passed on to new and legacy fund shareholders alike. This liability often comes as a surprise to investors who are already disappointed with a fund's performance. Because of the cyclical nature of the market, this situation happens much more often than you might imagine.

Gold ETFs are set up in such a way that their tax liability is similar to holding an individual stock; you pay taxes on your gains when you sell the shares, not when the managers make an adjustment to the fund's holdings. They also can be held within a tax-sheltered account such as a traditional or Roth IRA. What works best for you from a tax perspective will vary, and you should have a discussion about any significant changes to your portfolio, including a new position in a gold or gold stock ETF, with a professional advisor.

Liquidity

Mutual funds and other private managers are not very good at returning client assets. Some mutual funds charge fees for a withdrawal that can be high enough to erase gains and even create a loss, depending on the fund's performance and your holding period. This is a particularly frustrating problem if you need to make a change quickly and can lead to a no-win situation for individual investors who need access to their capital or want to make a change.

BULLION ETFs

The largest gold bullion ETF in the industry is the SPDR Gold Trust ETF (GLD), which owns gold bullion that is held in the vaults of the custodian HSBC, one of the largest of the so-called bullion banks. This fund is so massive that it is the sixth largest gold owner in the world with holdings of 1,291 tonnes, which is currently worth $57.6 billion. The only gold investors with larger holdings are the governments and central banks of the United States, Germany, France, and Italy and the IMF. That means that the fund has economies of scale (efficiency) and very high liquidity.

The fund is popular for many reasons, the most important of which is that it was one of the first to make low-cost gold bullion ownership through a fund accessible to a wide segment of the individual and institutional investor population. Buying shares of GLD means you don't need to hold gold physically and worry about storage costs, liquidity, and other issues. The fees are very low, and you can buy and sell the ETF like a regular stock in your brokerage account. In general we recommend GLD as a great long-term tool to hold gold bullion (despite a few flaws) and as one of the best choices for gold options traders because of its excellent liquidity. The interest in gold bullion ETFs such as GLD is one of several reasons we are forecasting that gold prices will continue to rise in the coming years. As large as it is, GLD and its new and emerging competitors have barely scratched the surface of the possible pool of gold investors. As more individuals and institutions arrive at the inevitable conclusion that to preserve capital in the new age of currency wars and quantitative easing they need some exposure to gold, demand will drive prices higher.

There are a few other gold bullion ETFs that are very similar to GLD, and we expect to see more introduced in the near term. As more ETFs are launched, we will continue to see downward pressure on fees (which are already quite low) and may see some improvements in transparency, which is one of the few gripes we have with GLD. One of the best alternatives to GLD is the iShares Gold Trust ETF (IAU), which offers lower fees, a lower share price, and better reporting. Smaller traders and long-term investors find the lower share price (one-tenth of GLD) and management cost (0.25 percent) very compelling reasons to prefer IAU to GLD. In principle, we agree that IAU is another step in the right direction for bullion ETFs, but the options on IAU are not as liquid as those on GLD and present problems for investors with more complicated strategies.

Other than costs, share prices, and options, there are a few differences between the major bullion ETFs, but they are not likely to be very material for most individual investors. The weaknesses of bullion ETFs are also very similar from fund to fund, although we wouldn't suggest that any of these flaws are fatal. For the most part, these issues are not unique to gold bullion ETFs, but you should understand what they are before making an investing decision.

Indexing Error

It will always be impossible to match the theoretical returns of an asset through an ETF, but if you include the costs inherent in holding physical gold bullion when you compare the performance of the asset and that of a low-cost ETF, the fund very likely will be a cheaper alternative. For the most part the indexing error can be explained as a combination of the costs to acquire and manage the gold inventory, issue shares, and pay management fees. In the case of bullion ETFs this difference will be fairly nominal. For example, as of this writing, IAU is up 26.19 percent over the last 12 months, GLD is up 26.21 percent, and bullion itself is up 26.36 percent. We expect the difference to grow somewhat larger over time as fees are charged by the ETFs, but it should still make a relatively small difference. Keep in mind that holding physical bullion is not cost- or risk-free.

Transparency

ETFs usually report their holdings through formal disclosures and from time to time on their Web sites, and there is often a small mismatch between what is shown in those reports and the current value of the fund. There are several reasons for this, but there is legitimate concern that investors may not have all the information they want. Periodically there are calls for more thorough audits and increased frequency of reports to the shareholders of these ETFs, and we expect that as competition matures, more transparency will become the norm. Gold investors tend to be a very demanding bunch when it comes to disclosure, so if this is a concern for you, it may be one more reason to prefer IAU to GLD because of a higher standard of reporting and auditing.

Credit Risk

Theoretically, an ETF is backed by its assets and therefore its shareholders are secure; however, the definition of assets, shares, and security can be a little hazier than one might think. It is possible for an ETF manager or sponsor to go out of business or defraud its shareholders. Shareholders in an ETF may not have the same rights in the event of a bankruptcy that would apply to stockholders in a public company. The bullion ETFs mentioned in this chapter have a very low risk of fraud or bankruptcy, but it has happened before and is another argument for diversification even within your gold holdings.

On a related note, although we have not discussed exchange-traded notes (ETNs) in this book, they are very similar to ETFs but carry much higher credit risk without any offsetting advantages. As a rule we suggest avoiding ETNs in the gold market.

Conflicts of Interest

We know that we can't get away with a discussion about bullion ETFs without at least a small nod to the conspiracy theories that circulate among gold investors. Gold bullion ETFs have custodian banks that hold the gold in their vaults. These banks are included in the list of bullion banks we discussed previously; HSBC is the custodian for GLD, and JPMorgan is the custodian for IAU. There are strange relationships between the large bullion banks and other major gold market participants such as the U.S. and European central banks. The banks don't disclose all their gold exposure and may be more aggressively leveraged than we know.

HSBC and JPMorgan are both notorious short gold traders in the futures market, and on the surface this makes it seem that the banks or custodians for the big ETFs are betting against their clients. This does seem weird, and some traders think that these large short positions artificially increase the supply of gold and keep prices lower than they would be otherwise. That may or may not be true, but the other side of the story is that the big banks could be short gold futures because they want to offset some exposure in long positions that are unreported. Unfortunately, we don't know, but as we discussed previously, if gold supplies are artificially high, more transparency in the future could drive prices that much higher.

GOLD STOCK ETFs

As a general rule, if you are a small investor, we recommend that you steer clear of holding individual stocks, and the same thing is true for gold stocks. Gold stock ETFs can solve this problem because they are highly liquid and offer a level of diversification that would be impossible for a small investor to replicate without significant costs. ETFs that index gold stocks can be a lot more volatile than gold bullion ETFs, but if you are inclined to take a little extra risk, gold stock ETFs offer a much higher potential return. A popular gold stock ETF that many traders favor is the Market Vectors Gold Miners ETF (GDX), which has a sister fund that may be even more interesting: the Market Vectors Junior Gold Miners ETF (GDXJ). Most investors assume that GDX covers the large-capitalization stocks within the industry and GDXJ covers the small stocks. To a certain extent that is true, but there is more to it.

GDX is focused primarily on U.S.-listed stocks, which limits its market exposure to mostly U.S. and Canadian firms. In addition, because the fund indexes gold miners on the basis of market capitalization, it is very heavily exposed to a few very large firms within the industry. By contrast, GDXJ is not as focused on small caps as one might suppose and has broader international coverage. This means that GDXJ has much better exposure to stocks that are listed in gold-producing nations with mature stock markets such as Australia and South Africa. The difference in international exposure is a good thing for two reasons. First, as a general rule, more diversification and less concentration is a good thing as long as it does not drive up costs, which is true in this case. Second, more exposure to stocks outside the United States helps offset your exposure to the value of the dollar. For example, assuming that the Australian dollar continues to gain against the U.S. dollar (not an unreasonable assumption) in the near term, Australian stocks held in the internationally focused ETF will benefit from that exposure.

Overall, you can assume that these two ETFs will differ in volatility, but the benefits of increased diversification and more exposure to small-cap firms would make GDXJ more attractive than GDX for an aggressive investor with a high risk tolerance. There are other gold-mining ETFs and mutual funds (Vanguard has a great one with very low costs), and a simple search at Morningstar.com can turn up several choices. The rules discussed previously for bullion ETFs also apply to the process of choosing a gold stock ETF. Concentrate on costs, liquidity, and transparency to make sure you are controlling things you have some ability to influence. You can't control the direction of the underlying market, but you can make sure you are minimizing other disadvantages, and in the long run concentrating on those factors can have a material impact on portfolio performance.

GOLD STOCKS

When traders talk about gold stocks or gold companies, they are referring to public firms that are actively producing gold or supplying property, plant, and equipment to gold miners. Many of the largest are in the United States and Canada and are listed on the major North American stock exchanges. The fundamentals of these firms look like the fundamentals of other public companies, and they can be analyzed against one another to determine relative performance just as one might approach an investment in any other industry group. For traders with a high risk tolerance and an adequate capital balance, gold stocks may be worth the effort as they can outperform both gold prices and gold stock ETFs in a bull market. The risks and potential rewards rise again once you move beyond the largest gold stocks and start looking at the category known as the "juniors." Junior gold stocks are smaller and much more speculative without solid track records of production, management, or profits, but a breakout can be very robust.

Gold Producers

Gold stocks track gold prices (more or less) but tend to have much more volatility, and within the group there can be some real shooting stars. For example, gold bullion prices have risen 25 percent over the last 12 months, but the largest of the gold producer stocks, Barrick Gold Corporation (ABX), is up over 32 percent. The potential for larger returns also carries extra risk, and at the bottom of the list of stocks we pulled for this analysis is a small cap called Jaguar Mining (JAG), which is down 37 percent over the last 12 months despite the bull market for gold. The firm is involved in exploration and production and clearly has not been as productive as investors thought it would be 12 months ago.

Within the gold investing industry, examples such as JAG often are used to "prove" why holding bullion outright is a better investment. Stocks such as NovaGold Resources (NG) usually are written off as a fluke or outlier that is impossible to replicate consistently. To a certain extent we agree with both of those arguments in that we don't know which stock in the gold sector will make 100 percent or lose 100 percent in a specific period, but we can be a little more confident about the entire sector on average. The average performance for the stocks within this sector over the last 12 months has been 36 percent, which is considerably better than that of bullion over the same period. Of course this argument is intentionally biased; no investor should base a decision to buy one thing over another solely on its most recent performance. How volatile the investment is, your personal risk tolerance, and your personal preferences are all important factors that we have ignored.

We made the argument this way because within the gold industry, analysts and advisors tend to be very polar about the best investments. Some suggest that because gold stocks are an indirect investment in gold and are subject to additional market risks, they are inferior to holding bullion; on the other side, stock investors suggest that because gold won't appreciate in value from an improvement in processing or discoveries, it will lag the market and is a flawed investment. Both sides of this argument are right and both are wrong; the answer lies in your personal portfolio objectives. Imagine an investor who has been allocated 80 percent in the stock of the S&P 500 and 20 percent in gold bullion for the last 10 years. Over that period this investor is up 75 percent on her portfolio, whereas the S&P is actually down almost 14 percent over the period. An investor with an identical allocation in the S&P 500 and the remaining 20 percent in an index of gold stocks would be up over 100 percent. However, the ride was a lot rougher and there were times the gold stock investor was down much more than the bullion investor.

This example is important to think about because looking back, it's easy to say that gold stocks were superior, but that comes with hindsight. Toward the end of 2008, the situation was much different and the bullion investor would have been feeling pretty smart. In the end, the decision is about what you are after as an investor. Gold will be less volatile than gold stocks, and that is important for an investor with a priority on capital preservation, whereas gold stocks are likely to be more attractive to an investor looking for both diversification and aggressive opportunities for growth. As you look at some of the characteristics (and flaws) of the best gold and gold stock ETFs in the market, consider what kind of investor you are before making a decision. For the purposes of this book we are taking a more neutral stance on which is best in order to concentrate on some of the pitfalls you need to watch out for and what benefits matter most.

Junior Gold Producers

Usually the definition of gold juniors includes new and/or small companies. These stocks tend to be volatile and risky, but we don't consider them bad investments if you fully understand the risks associated with them. In a way they are similar to making an investment in a biotech firm or a new technology company. The potential is large, the investment required is small, but the risk is great; this is another illustration of the relationship between risk and potential reward. A currently popular junior gold stock is NovaGold (NG), a Canadian firm that is focused on exploration. This company will be a greater risk than a large-cap stock or gold bullion itself because it has a more difficult time projecting actual production and may be subject to serious price shocks. In 2007, NG dropped from a high price of $21.91 a share in November to $5.87 by the end of December. However, over the last 12 months, bullion is up only 25 percent and large gold stocks are up 27 percent, but NG is up 180 percent, having partially recovered from the 2007 debacle.

The trade-off between risk and reward is unavoidable, and you will see it in the junior subsector. Diversification through an ETF or by spreading your risk across several junior gold stocks can help reduce potential volatility, but it ultimately will be a personal decision. Gold stocks are not a one-size-fits-all opportunity, but with the proper education and a little research they represent a very profitable way to outperform the price of gold. In the strategies section of the book we will discuss some of the ways options traders can exercise even more control over the amount of risk they are taking when buying a junior gold stock.

STOCK OPTIONS

There is definitely more than one way to get some gold exposure into your portfolio. Although we highly recommend both bullion and gold stocks (or bullion and gold stock ETFs for liquidity and low costs), active investors who really want flexibility and maximum control need to know how to use options. In this section we will explain why this is true and get you started on becoming a gold options trader in addition to being a gold investor. We will discuss only vanilla options (calls and puts) on exchange-traded products such as ETFs and stocks. There are also vanilla options available on gold futures, but there isn't an inherent advantage for individual investors in using futures options over stock options, and for small traders they can be difficult to access. There are other options styles available in the gold market that sometimes are referred to as exotic options; however, as far as we can tell, the term "exotic" is merely a euphemism for "higher costs" and "wider spread." Needless to say, exotic options are not recommended.

There is an important misconception about the risk of trading options that we should get out of the way at the beginning of the section. We find that many traders are a little nervous about using these products in the gold market because they assume that buying calls or puts is riskier than buying stock or ETF shares outright. It is true that options are leveraged products, which means that they can be more risky, but they are also very flexible and can be used to reduce risk and account volatility. The split personality of options is what makes them such an effective tool for gold traders; they are as risky (or safe) as you make them.

We will cover a few of the basics of options trading strategies in the gold market in this section and will use options as a product to execute some of the strategy case studies later in the book. If you are already familiar with options, this section will be a little basic, so feel free to skip ahead, but if you are new to options, don't worry: We have some extra resources to help you to learn more. Like most investment products, options require a learning curve, so if you are starting from scratch, don't get buried in the details. See if the strategies we detail in the book are something you find interesting. If they are, you can start learning more about options and practice making trades without having to pay a dime or risk anything in your portfolio.

The Options Industry Council (a trade association supported by options brokers in the United States) runs a Web site with several free courses on options trading. Go to www.888options.com and register for a few courses. They have done an excellent job, and it's a great place to get started. The CBOE (Chicago Board Options Exchange) also offers free courses on options trading, and there are three top-of-the-line paper trading applications you can use free of charge to put some strategies to the test before you attempt anything in your live account. You can access those courses and software at www.cboe.com.

Call Options

When you buy a call option, you have the right to buy the underlying stock for a specific price (the strike price) at some point in the future. A call option expires, but you can choose how much time you want before expiration as well as the strike price you want. If you buy a call option, you can sell it tomorrow or any day before expiration. If you buy a call option today and gold prices move up tomorrow, that call probably will be more valuable as well and you could sell it for a profit. A call option eventually expires, and at that time it can be exercised; that means you can buy the stock that the option represents at the strike price. However, very few retail traders choose to exercise their options because it is almost always cheaper and easier to sell an option for a profit before it expires.

Example of Buying a Call

On November 16, 2010, the SPDR Gold Trust ETF (GLD) was priced at $130.97 per share. The gold market had recently pulled back to support as the dollar strengthened because concerns about the European debt crisis were high and there had been a lot of uncertainty about the potential actions of the Chinese central bank to tighten monetary policy. A situation like this would seem to be very favorable for gold, but a stronger dollar can be a bad thing for gold prices. Subsequently GLD was at support and seemed like a potential reentry opportunity for gold bulls.

As a gold bull, you can choose to buy the stock or you can buy a call option instead. This will provide leverage because the option represents 100 shares and will cost much less than the stock itself. Assume that you think a gold rally will happen in the short term, and so you don't need to pay for a very long expiration date. In this case, you decide to purchase the $131 strike price call with expiration in January. That option will cost $4.75 per share, or $475 per contract of 100 shares. This means that you have the right to buy the stock any time before the January 2011 expiration (the third

Friday of the month) for $131 per share. By January 3, 2011, GLD has rallied and the ETF is now priced at 138.72 per share. It turned out that your forecast was right (lucky you!), and you are now in a profitable trade. The call option at this point is worth $8.00 per share, or $800 per contract, because you still have the right to buy the stock for the strike price at $131 per share plus a little remaining time value. To harvest your profits, you don't need to exercise the option and buy the stock; you can just sell the call for $800 per contract and walk away with the profits.

When traders talk about option leverage, they are talking about the ability to benefit from a large move in the underlying stock without having to make a large investment in absolute dollar terms. If you had purchased 100 shares of GLD on November 16 rather than the call, it would have required an investment of $13,097, but instead you purchased the call option for $475 for the right to "control" 100 shares of stock. Buying the stock itself would have returned 6 percent, or you would have profited 68 percent with the call option. Leverage is a two-edged sword because although you invested less in absolute dollar terms, if the market drops, you could lose up to 100 percent of what you invested in that call option. This example was meant to provide a short illustration of how call options work. If you buy a call option like this, you are taking extra risk (a leveraged trade is always more risky than an unleveraged trade) but have the potential for a higher reward as well. As we dig into the details behind some effective gold options strategies later in the book, you will learn more about why options can also reduce risk in your portfolio; they are not just for aggressive traders looking for big moves in the short term.

Put Options

When you buy a put, you are making an investment that will grow in value if the underlying ETF or gold stock drops. Traders often purchase puts for insurance against their long positions in gold rather than because they think gold prices will drop in the short term. That strategy works because the put will gain in value as the long position in gold falls in price, which will partially offset the loss in the investment. This is often referred to as a protective put, and it is a common trade for large institutional traders. Buying a put is also a simple way to profit from a decline in gold prices as a speculator, and many short-term traders take positions like this periodically when the market for gold gets overheated and a short-term trend to the downside emerges.

A put gives you the right to sell the underlying gold stock or ETF at the put's strike price any time before it expires. Very few traders actually exercise a put, and because the gold market is so liquid, there is generally no difficulty selling a put for a profit before expiration. Opening a put trade by selling to open or short-ing the put (sometimes called put writing) is also a very effective strategy for traders who want to buy a gold ETF or stock for less than its current price should the stock's price retrace slightly. That strategy is simple to execute and is one of the most effective long-term strategies for active investors willing to take a moderate amount of risk.

Example of Buying a Put

On December 4, 2009, the price of gold began to pull back quickly from the all-time highs set just a few days before. As the decline accelerated, put buyers began to move into bearish positions to protect their gains or speculate on the decline in gold. At the time the SPDR Gold Trust ETF (GLD) was priced at $113.75, having dropped from $119.50 just a few days before. A bearish trader could have shorted the stock or bought a put, but buying the put pro-vides extra leverage and, depending on the situation, may actually be a better trade than an outright short of the ETF. There are a few specific reasons for this that we will discuss later in the book. Keep in mind that buying a put is not just a way to profit by being a gold bear or contrarian; it's a great way to protect the profits within your long-term gold holdings when you are concerned about a decline in the market.

At the time, an at-the-money put at the $114 strike price with a February 2010 expiration date was worth $4.56 per share, or $456 per contract. If gold prices continued to fall, that put could become worth a lot more, or if it turned out that the forecast was wrong and gold resumed its prior upward trend immediately, the maximum risk was the price paid for the put. Keep in mind that when you buy an option, you can sell it any time you wish, so if it turns out that the forecast was wrong, the put could have been sold early to cut the losses short. Prices had fallen to $106 before February's expiration, and the put could have been sold for at least $8 (the difference between the stock price and the strike price) per share, or $800 per contract. That is a tidy gain of 75 percent on the amount originally invested.

As we mentioned above, although some speculators may wish to profit from a decline in gold by buying puts, other traders may buy them to cover or insure against potential losses. Consider in the previous example a trader who held GLD as a long-term investment but decided that the potential downside after the breakout in December was too large and that she needed some protection. She may have decided to insure against her loss with a long put, which would have prevented her from losing a much larger amount because the gains on the put would have offset most of the loss in the longer-term position in GLD. In this way, the protective put acted like a stop-loss without the risk of being "whipped" out of the position with a very short-term spike to the downside that is erased a few days later.

Traders who buy a protective put can remove that protection at any time, and since the put won't offset their gains by more than the original purchase price, it is ideal for investors looking for a temporary hedge when market volatility gets a little extreme. Our objective in this contrasting example was to help you understand how to use gold options to be more flexible as a trader. In the strategies section of the book we will go into much more specific detail about setting up trades like this and how to manage them over time.

FUTURES

Based on total dollar volume, gold futures are more liquid than any other gold product besides bullion itself. Despite that liquidity, we debated whether to include futures in the products category because they require a significant learning curve and a large account to trade effectively. However, for active traders, gold futures are cost-efficient and can be adapted to any of the strategies we will discuss in the book. Even if you decide not to use futures to invest in gold, knowing how they work is important because you will understand how analysts and the press talk about gold prices and some of the underlying fundamentals in the market. Many of the largest gold traders in the world use futures extensively, and because large positions and trades are reported by the futures exchanges, this can help us understand more about what the big money is doing in the market.

If you are a United States–based investor, the gold futures you will be using are traded on the exchanges in Chicago and New York, and, like stocks, gold futures contracts can be traded electronically through an online brokerage account. We will go into more detail later in this section about finding and evaluating good futures brokers and charting applications. It is even possible to hold a futures account with the same broker you use for stocks, options, and ETFs.

What Is a Futures Contract?

A futures contract is essentially an agreement between a buyer and a seller to complete a gold transaction for a fixed price at some point in the future. Most gold futures contracts represent 100 ounces, but there is also a popular mini-version that is 33 ounces in size and recently a 10-ounce micro contract has become available.

When you buy a futures contract, you are essentially promising to buy 100 ounces of gold at the current futures price at expiration. As the futures buyer or seller you are obligated to complete the transaction if you hold the contract through expiration. This is a lot like exercising in the options market, but it is very rare for a futures buyer to actually "take delivery" or for a futures seller to "make delivery" of the gold at the end of the contract. Usually the contract is sold or bought back to close the transaction for a profit well before expiration. Most futures brokers won't even allow delivery to happen, and unless you tell them otherwise, they will close the trade in your account before expiration unless you do it yourself.

If you were bearish on gold, you could be the gold futures seller and agree to sell gold at expiration for the current futures price. As the seller, you will profit if gold drops and the contract becomes less valuable because you can buy it back later for a cheaper price. You could also be the gold futures buyer if you believe that gold prices are likely to go up in the future. Imagine that gold futures are priced today at $1,200 an ounce and you believe they will go up to $1,350 in the next three months. If you buy the contract today and your forecast is correct, you will profit $150 per ounce, which is a return of 12 percent on the cash value of the contract. Like options, futures are leveraged and require margin rather than the entire cash value of the contract, and so the actual return would be much larger than 12 percent.

A futures trader posts "margin" or a deposit with his broker that is a portion or fraction of the futures contract value, which means that the trader can control a large amount of gold for a small amount of dollars. The minimum margin requirement to buy one gold futures contract varies with the broker, but right now the standard to control a full gold contract is 4 to 6 percent of a future's value. In the example above you would need to post margin of $4,800 to $7,200 to buy or sell one full-size (100 ounces) futures contract. The leverage, or "gearing," that margin provides turns the 12 percent gain into a 312 percent gain at the lowest margin level. This is what gets many traders excited about gold futures, but remember that leverage can cut both ways. If gold falls in value, you would lose more than your initial margin requirement and would have to keep allocating additional cash to your margin deposit to stay in the trade. This was an extreme example, but you get the basic idea.

The process works basically the same way if you are a futures seller. If you sold a gold futures contract at $1,200 and the price fell to $1,000 an ounce, you would still have the right to deliver bullion for $1,200 and therefore would have made a profit of $200 an ounce. Before expiration arrives you can buy the contract to close the trade and realize a profit. In fact, there are many futures buyers and sellers who will hold a contract for only a few days or even a few hours before taking their profits (or losses) off the table. The margin requirement for futures sellers works the same way that it does for buyers, and you will need to post 4 to 6 percent of the value of the contract in order to sell or "short" a contract. Margin is a minimum requirement, so if your forecast is wrong and you start accumulating losses, you will need to allocate more money to that margin deposit to prevent the contract from being closed. If losses become larger and the margin requirement (margin plus losses) is larger than the total amount in your account, you will have to deposit more money; this is referred to as a margin call.

It is possible to lose more than you had planned in the futures market as prices can move very quickly. In fact, if you overleverage your trades and a large price move takes place, you could lose more than you had in the entire account. This situation does happen from time to time with inexperienced traders, and the futures broker who gave you the account originally will want to collect the negative balance.

Advantages of Futures

There are several advantages of futures over other types of investments in gold.

Transparency and No Counterparty Risk

Futures are similar to the OTC gold lots we discussed in the bad products category; however, they don't have the same disadvantages and counterparty risks. That means that the other side of your trade is not the futures broker. Futures are traded on an exchange; this provides transparency behind pricing and should make you feel much more confident that the other side of the transaction doesn't have more information or control over the trade than you do. Transparency also means that you can see volume and order flow data; that is important for many technical traders but is unavailable in the OTC gold market.

Tax Advantages

Futures traders get some preferential tax benefits because futures are a Section 1256 (U.S. tax code) product. That means that gains are taxed (no matter how long you held the contract) as 40 percent short-term and 60 percent long-term capital gains, which is not true for stocks or gold ETFs. Also, all your futures transactions can be lumped together onto a single 1099 at the end of the year, which is something that very active stock and options traders immediately recognize as a benefit compared with filling out the details of an entire year's worth of trading activity on a Schedule D (U.S. tax form).

Liquidity and Availability

We have discussed how massive the largest gold ETF in the world is, yet its daily volume is a mere fraction of the daily notional value that is traded in the gold futures market. Currently almost seven times the value of gold is traded through the Chicago and New York exchanges than through gold ETFs on a daily basis. That translates into tight spreads, fast execution, and superior availability, all of which can reduce costs for very short-term traders.

Futures trade Sunday through Friday from 6:00 p.m. until 5:15 p.m. the next day. That means you can make a trade in the gold futures market when the stock market is closed. If you are an extremely active trader with a full-time job outside the financial markets, this may be a significant advantage. Because of the global nature of the gold market, plenty of liquidity and trading opportunities are available day and night.

Disadvantages of Futures

Futures also have a number of disadvantages that need to be considered.

Learning Curve

If you want to learn to invest in gold the easy way, futures are not the solution because it takes effort to learn how to buy or sell the contracts and how to open and fund a brokerage account. However, thousands of traders work in the futures market every day because the benefits can be well worth the effort required. If you decide to investigate futures further, you should start by opening a paper trading account so that you can practice without putting any money at risk.

Contango and Carrying Costs

Gold futures exist in a near-perpetual state of contango, which means that contracts with a longer expiration cost more than those with a shorter expiration. That means that when you sell one futures contract before it expires and buy the next one with a longer expiration, you are locking in a small loss. Long-term investors who don't anticipate making changes to their portfolios very often will probably do better by investing in a low-cost bullion ETF or physical bullion itself.

Inflexibility

The most popular futures contracts require a significant margin deposit, and so you may be priced out of the market while you acquire more assets. If this is an issue for you, it would be a mistake to take on larger positions just because there aren't futures contracts small enough to accommodate your account. There are several alternatives for leverage that can be used while you build your balance.

HOW TO PICK THE RIGHT STOCK/FUTURES BROKER

We have both worked on the brokerage side of the business as employees and consultants, and through those experiences we have learned a lot about how that side of the trading business is run and why it has been changing as the market matures. We will be drawing from that experience throughout this section to help you understand what really matters to a brokerage and its clients. This is an important question for new gold traders because the right broker can help you reduce costs while improving market access. How to choose the right broker is one of the most common questions we get at our Web site, but the truth is that there really isn't a "best" broker. There are some who are very good and there are a few who are really bad, but which one is really the best will vary with who you are as a trader. What we will do throughout this section is help you think through the research you can do on your own to cut through all the marketing and determine for yourself who the best brokerage or brokerages are for you. Before we dig into the factors that matter most, let's cut through some of the marketing myths the industry would like you to believe.

Choosing a Broker Is Not Like Proposing Marriage

There are many traders out there who find themselves in a situation in which they feel a little stuck or constrained in their accounts. Most brokers tend to specialize in a specific kind of trader by offering compelling commissions, services, and fees that address a very narrow set of strategies or products. For example, there are several great brokerages that offer commission-free trading in gold ETFs but charge excessive fees to execute an options trade. That may be great if you are investing exclusively in ETFs or other long-term positions, but if you want to expand your strategic alternatives, costs can be a big constraint. Similarly, there are several excellent brokerages that specialize in low costs for active options and futures traders but charge too much when you need to make a change to a longer-term holding. Therefore, we suggest that unless you fit the description of the ideal account for a particular broker, you should consider the advantages of spreading your assets around by using more than one firm.

Being willing to diversify by trading with more than one broker allows you to optimize your costs on the basis of trading strategies more effectively and gives you broader access to trading tools and information. Brokers know that maintaining more than one account is not uncommon, and it is an effective way for you send your broker the important message that you are an independent trader. Knowing that her customers are mobile will motivate a broker to improve service and reduce costs to compete and keep them as customers. Your bargaining power with a broker is probably much greater than you think. It costs an average of $1,000 to acquire a brokerage account in the United States; therefore, most firms are highly motivated to retain your account once it has been established.

Advertised Rates Are Meaningless

Brokers are required to disclose commissions and fees in their marketing materials, but those costs vary much more than one would think. Many fees and charges are hidden, and the rates that are advertised in the ubiquitous comparison table are cherry-picked to make each broker look better than his competitors. We will go into more detail about this later, but we always suggest that in evaluating a broker you should ignore the advertised, or "rack," rates and start negotiating.

Reviews Are Biased and Incomplete

Big financial periodicals or online publications "rate" and "review" brokers in annual or quarterly issues. The problem is that they are essentially reviewing their biggest advertisers and you are getting the opinion of an author who probably doesn't trade because of conflicts of interest (most employed financial journalists are not allowed to trade). Often brokers are required to pay the magazine or publication to be included in the review process, and it is hard to imagine that those payments don't influence results.

The problem here is that one size does not fit all in the brokerage business; therefore, even if the review wasn't paid for or biased in some way, it isn't very relevant to you. Traders willing to do a little work on their own rather than reading reviews are much less likely to discover nasty surprises on the first brokerage statement.

They All Have Terrible Service

There are a variety of reasons for the uniformly bad service in the brokerage business, but there isn't much you can do to change it. It may be tempting to assume that because you are a sophisticated trader service isn't a big issue, but when you need to get someone on the phone, it is probably going to be for something urgent. We get questions from readers and industry analysts about this problem all the time and it's easy to blame it on regulations or smaller margins (which has certainly contributed to the problem), but the blame probably rests with account holders who don't investigate brokerage service departments until after they have set up an account. Before you opened your most recent account, you probably compared commissions and downloaded the trading application, but did you call the service department? If you did, you are in the minority. Brokerages know this, and so they don't make it a priority; however, there are a few easy tests you can use to investigate a brokerage service department before making a decision.

Due Diligence

Imagine that you were considering giving a stranger access to your bank accounts. What would you want to know about that person before you did that? Is he trustworthy? Is he in need of money and thus tempted to steal yours? Does he lie or mislead others? These are the same questions you should ask when you investigate a new broker or gold dealer because those people actually are strangers and you really are giving them access to your bank accounts.

It's very easy to research a licensed brokerage before opening an account. If you are researching a United States–based dealer or futures broker, the NFA (National Futures Association) lists the registered representatives and the firms they work for within the "BASIC" system, which is available from its online home page at nfa.futures.org. Try it yourself and look up both the names of the people you talk to on the phone at your futures brokerage and the firm itself. You will find out if their registration is current, what licenses they hold, and if there have been any complaints or actions taken against them or the firm. You may be surprised by what you find.

The Financial Industry Regulatory Authority (FINRA) has very similar information available for individuals researching stock brokers and brokerages. You can access its search feature, "BrokerCheck," from its home page at finra.org. You should ask questions about disputes or disciplinary actions (if there are any) that have been taken before making a decision. The way the brokerage's representatives respond to these questions about their regulatory history will tell you a lot about the culture of the firm and the knowledge level of the person you are talking to.

We always suggest that the most important part of your due diligence is to call and start asking questions. It is shocking how common it is for an investor to apply for a brokerage account and begin transferring money online without even considering making a phone call or visiting the office locally. We recommend that you call your prospective broker several times to get a feel for how quickly she picks up the phone, the accuracy of the answers, and the knowledge level of the first line of support. You should call during high-volume hours in the market and after the market has closed to see what kind of availability they offer and whether service levels change. If you are drawing a blank for what kinds of questions to ask, here are a few suggestions to get you started:

- "Hi, can you tell me what the expense ratio for GLD is and if you expect that it will change in the near term?"
- "What is the initial margin requirement today for the mini-gold futures contract? Does that requirement change overnight, and if so, what will it be?"
- "Will you allow me to short a put option in my account? What is the margin requirement if I want to short an at-the-money put on GDX?"
- "If I buy options on a gold index option like GOX, will those gains be subject to 60/40 percent tax treatment or will it all be short-term capital gains?"
- "What are the commission rates to buy shares of an ETF like GLD if I call you on the phone to do it versus entering the order online?"

Calling to ask questions is the fastest way to put a brokerage to the test, and the differences from one broker to the next will stand out. The balance of power has shifted from the broker to the client over the last decade as the popularity of online trading platforms has grown. This has been a difficult transition for the industry, so you shouldn't expect satisfactory responses from everyone.

Two Easy Steps to Get the Best Commissions
There is very little about the gold market that traders can control, and that means that factors you can influence should be maximized (or, in the case of commissions, minimized). Investing products are uniform from one brokerage to the next (a stock is a stock), and so commissions are one of the few things a brokerage can

adjust to attract your account dollars. It would seem that a straight-forward comparison of broker commissions would easily show who the low-commission leader is, but that is not the case. Commission comparison tables are misleading, and advertised rates don't show everything you may have to pay depending on your account size and activity level.

The brokers are not technically lying about their advertised commissions, but they are doing a lot of cherry-picking to make their rates look the best. This means that most brokerages are showing only select commissions and trade sizes that will make them look better against a few of their competitors. They may offer the best commission rate for buying 100 shares of a gold ETF but be hiding the fact that they have the highest commission for buying call options. For example, we regularly do surveys of the leading online brokers just to see what is going on in the industry. Recently, the lowest commission among the major brokers to trade 100 shares of a gold ETF was a flat $2.95 per trade and the highest commission was $10 per trade. On the basis of that information alone, the low-cost leader seems like a compelling choice, but what isn't obvious is that if you are an extremely active gold trader, another competitor will charge only $1.00 per trade. They also didn't mention that if you are not a very active trader there are several excellent brokers who will let you trade up to three times per month for no charge.

Looking at brokers' cost comparison tables has very little meaning. They are heavily footnoted and are usually biased toward a narrow style of trading or account size. To get the best commissions you need to look at it from the other direction by thinking about your needs before you even glance at a commission comparison table. Starting with that process, here are two specific things you can do to make sure you are getting the very best commission rates from your broker.

Evaluate and Record Your Typical Trading Needs and Size. Before you can compare costs, you have to know who you are as an investor or trader, so before you conduct any comparisons, write down what you are trading, how frequently you execute an order or modify one, and how often you make adjustments, deposits, or withdrawals from your account. You will also need to define what your account size is now and how quickly it is growing and whether you need to set up an IRA or access other account services. This information will form the basis for your custom survey of brokerage costs. This is a very important activity because it is the only way to determine the total cost of your account.

Brokers don't just charge commissions; they also charge account fees and collect interest on margin. These fees vary a lot and can make a big difference to your overall profitability. For example, currently the average margin interest rate is hovering around 7 percent in the industry, which is a lot like the interest rate of a midquality credit card; however, the best margin rates are closer to 2 percent. Similarly, some brokers pay interest on your deposits and others pay nothing; although this isn't a fee, it could make a big difference if you are trading a large account and frequently have a cash balance. Account fees are not as obvious as commissions and can include statement fees, activity fees, check fees, transfer fees, and debit card and checking account fees, among others, that can all really add up. One of the largest publicly listed discount brokers revealed in its 2009 annual report that it made almost as much in fees and interest on client accounts as it did in commissions during the year. This is not unusual, and if the broker can avoid having to address your specific needs, you are less likely to realize what it is charging you.

Once you know what you look like as an investor and what kinds of costs you may have to pay, it's time to do a little research; however, do not do this by going to a brokerage's Web site. That won't answer your questions completely, and this is another opportunity to complete your due diligence. Take your list of trades and transactions as well as the description of you as a trader to all the brokers you are interested in and have them tell you what the total cost will be per month and per year. We can assure you that there are very few clients who ask for this kind of feedback. Some brokers you investigate will refuse to discuss fees in detail or to negotiate, which is fine because a refusal is a valuable answer that tells you something about what working with that broker would be like.

Doing research like this forces the broker to address you as an individual rather than an account number, and you want to establish an individual relationship with your brokerage right from the beginning. The answers you get from brokers willing to respond to your request will surprise you if you compare them with the advertised rates. Some companies that looked expensive in the beginning may be much cheaper than other competitors when all costs are accounted for and your unique needs are addressed.

Ask for a Better Commission Rate. The consumer culture in the United States is such that it is very uncommon to attempt to negotiate prices except on very large items such as a car, a home, or jewelry; therefore, traders rarely ask for better rates or costs from their brokers. An individual commission may be low, but over a year, those fees are quite significant and the commissions and fees listed in the disclosures or marketing materials (rack rates) are not the lowest commissions available. Depending on your account size and activity level, a good brokerage will be willing to negotiate a better cost structure to get your business but won't volunteer to negotiate; you have to ask.

There are a few companies that refuse to negotiate, but most will and they are often willing to negotiate individual items or the whole package of fees and costs. For example, a common policy in the brokerage industry is to be willing to match the published rates of another broker. For instance, assume you really like Broker A because it offers great tools and you can trade both gold ETFs and futures within the same platform; Broker B is a lot cheaper but doesn't offer the same products or tools. You should try asking Broker A to match Broker B's rates because chances are very good that she will be willing to get close enough to make a deal. This is also another great opportunity to establish the priorities in your broker-client relationship. Brokers work for you, not the other way around.

Is Your Brokerage Account Protected?

Most brokerage accounts are insured in a similar way to the way bank accounts are protected; however, not all accounts are insured, and that insurance has limits. This is obviously not something that will have to be called on very often, but if you need it and it isn't there, it's an account killer. There isn't much that you need to know about account insurance, but it is a good topic of conversation with the brokers you are investigating. Stock and option brokerages carry insurance from the SIPC (Securities Investor Protection Corporation) to cover your account in case you suffer losses during liquidation; however, the SIPC covers only assets that are lost. If your brokerage goes out of business, most of your assets probably will be returned to you (eventually), and the SIPC will step in only to make you whole on assets that can't be returned. Even then, it covers only up to $500,000 in additional losses.

Many traders are surprised to find out that some accounts don't even have this minimum level of protection. Gold bullion dealers and OTC firms often carry no insurance at all on your account. Other brokers may insure most accounts but maintain special account categories for things such as gold investments that are not insured. For example, in October 2005 one of the largest futures brokerages (Refco) in the United States announced that the CEO had hidden $430 million in bad debts and had disappeared. The company was effectively insolvent, and although most account holders only needed to wait for their assets to be returned and SIPC insurance to kick in, there was a segmented class of traders who lost everything because their accounts were completely unprotected.

What Refco had done by not insuring those special retail accounts was not technically illegal or against regulations, but that made little difference to the account holders. Talk to your broker about what happens if they become insolvent and find out if your account is insured and, if so, whether it is just the minimum or if they have purchased additional coverage. It is no longer safe to assume that Wall Street firms will remain solvent indefinitely. As an account holder you need to know how you are covered and what happens if the firm runs into trouble.

International Accounts

We get questions all the time about whether it is possible to hold a United States–based brokerage account to trade exchange-listed gold products even if you don't live there. Most brokers are willing to take international accounts, and a quick phone call will tell you whether that is possible. Customer service can tell you about any additional requirements that may apply to you, but in general, if you don't live in the United States, the process of setting up an account is pretty simple and takes only a few weeks to complete.

International accounts need to fill out the traditional brokerage account application and a form for the U.S. Treasury (IRS Form W-8), which identifies you as a non-U.S. resident. This form usually has to be returned to the broker in hard-copy format and can take a little time, but it isn't a big issue. The form is only about a page long and should take five minutes or less to complete. Brokerages also send out a tax form at the end of the year to all their accounts called a 1099 that is almost always prepared by a third party who won't bother to differentiate between domestic and foreign accounts. If you get one of these, you should seek local professional help to determine how your trading activities affect your tax liability in your native jurisdiction.

BULLION

For some gold investors there is no substitute for physical ownership. Besides the profit potential of a bull market, theoretically,
holding the physical asset protects you against credit risk and the
mild uncertainty inherent in gold bullion ETFs, deposits, futures,
and funds. However, you will have to pay the costs of storage or
bear the risk of holding the asset in your physical possession.
Although there are trade-offs, holding gold bullion still offers a
level of control and direct exposure to the market that some
investors find very attractive, and when it is done right, the disadvantages can be minimized. There are several different forms of
gold bullion products (including bars and coins) that we will discuss next, but for the most part the best products are probably a
matter of personal preference.

Gold Coins

We have already discussed some of the problems in the gold coin
market; however, if you avoid the issues associated with having to
determine the "collectible" component of a coin's value, it may be
a good solution. You can do this by working with an experienced
dealer in person and buying newly minted coins from a legitimate
source. A good dealer will charge you a premium of 4 to 6 percent
over the coin's melt value, but by working with the seller in person
you can avoid many other charges and risks associated with mail-
order companies. We recently did a short survey of some good
dealers offering gold American Buffalo one-ounce coins (99.9999
percent pure, issued by the U.S. Mint) for an average of $1,424 per
coin when the gold spot price was $1,362 an ounce. That is not a
terrible markup, but it will still take 18 years to break even on the
costs compared with the iShares bullion ETF (IAU) or 11 years
compared with the SPDR Gold ETF (GLD).

There are advertisements and television commercials from gold coin companies that we suggest should be avoided. Their markup is almost always much higher than that of a good dealer (25 percent or more is typical), and you may be setting yourself up for a hard sell when you call to order. We suggest that one of the best ways to buy gold coins is from a dealer you can visit in person, and a list of such dealers is available on the U.S. Mint's Web site at www.usmint.gov. Call around and make sure you are getting a fair quote and then go pick up the coins yourself. This saves you shipping, and you can make sure that the dealer is not just a fly-by-night post office box behind a magazine advertisement. Buying a gold or silver coin this way is easy, and you are more likely to have some recourse and leverage with the firm if something goes wrong. Visiting a dealer in person is also a great way to get educated about the process you will have to go through if you ever decide to sell your coins, which can be difficult if you don't know how the coin market works. Overall, coins are convenient and easy to store, which is why many traders prefer them.

Gold Bullion

Gold bars or ingots can be purchased in weights from a few grams to full 400-troy-ounce bars (the standard trading unit for gold bullion). The purity of gold bars varies from 99.5 percent pure, which is standard, to 99.999 percent at the high end. The price will vary with the size and purity, but bars can be acquired from a dealer the way coins can, and in many cases the coin dealers the U.S. Mint lists on its Web site are also bullion bar dealers.

If you decide that holding the physical asset is important to you, keep in mind that there will be a markup on the price of the gold bars you purchase. How much that markup is will vary, but making larger purchases and using more established dealers usually result in a smaller premium over gold's spot price. Do not fall for dealers offering gold at the spot price or below, because this is without question a scam and they will rip you off. There are a lot of dealers and private mints running schemes like that, and it is easy to be fooled unless you know what you are doing.

Before you make bullion or coin purchases, you should conduct your due diligence just as you would with a stock or futures broker. Talk to other customers, especially anyone who has sold his gold back to the dealer. If you are planning to make a major purchase, a legitimate dealer should be happy to provide reference accounts. It is also a good idea to check the firm with your state's department of commerce and the Better Business Bureau. Whether you decide on coins or bars, make sure you are prepared to deal with storage and insurance, especially for a large amount. We regularly see news stories about thieves who seem exceptionally good at finding the gold a homeowner has stashed. Gold coins are particularly difficult to recover after a theft because they usually are not individually numbered and can be sold through the mail or over the Internet with no questions asked.

Gold Bullion Storage

It is not only possible but probably preferable to buy bullion from a firm that offers audited and vaulted storage. There are several companies that do this, and it is much more convenient for a long-term investor. In most cases you can request delivery of your gold if you ever want it shipped to you, and you can buy and sell it back to the firm for regularly published prices. Because they audit and inventory your gold on site, there are no shipping issues and buying and selling the bullion is simpler and more transparent. For example, BullionVault is a firm that specializes in selling and storing small individual positions in gold and silver. BullionVault audits the gold held by investors on a daily basis, and any bars you purchase are considered a "bailment," which means that BullionVault is not allowed to leverage the gold the way banks do and the gold can't be liquidated if the firm goes out of business. The gold is actually owned by you, not by the firm. There are a few other companies like this, but it is a business model that is just emerging, so there isn't a lot of competition.

BullionVault charges 0.8 percent commission when you buy or sell (roughly four years' worth of fees if you bought an equivalent amount of gold ETF shares), and storage costs are 0.12 percent or $48 minimum per year. When put together, it is more expensive than bullion ETFs, but you actually own the gold in the vault, where it is audited, secure, and insured, which may be worth the cost. The process to invest is simple and can be done online. Doing your due diligence on a large firm like this is relatively easy and transparent. We picked this firm as a good example because it has targeted small retail customers. That focus has paid off, and the company has been growing exponentially over the last few years. It recently closed a round of financing from the World Gold Council for 12.5 million British pounds. If you are shopping for a turnkey solution for buying and owning gold without having to take the risk of storing it yourself, a firm like BullionVault is a market leader.

There are banks that offer similar services, but make sure you understand the difference between allocated gold that actually is owned by you and unallocated gold that you don't really own and that can be leveraged by the bank. There are a lot of gold traders out there who are very surprised to find that they have been paying a bank for gold that they thought existed and was allocated to them but was in fact part of an unallocated pool of bullion. For example, Morgan Stanley was sued in 2009 for charging customers to acquire, store, and audit gold that may not have existed. The bank settled out of court without admitting the charges, but most analysts in the business have assumed the plaintiff's claims were true and that the practice is widespread within the industry.

We should disclose again that we are not big fans of physical gold ownership because it drives up costs. No matter how you do it, bullion will always be less liquid, less flexible, and more expensive to own in the short term than the other instruments we have discussed in this book. We think the risks of indirect gold ownership (ETFs and futures) are often overstated whereas the very real risks of holding physical gold bullion are routinely underestimated by individual investors; however, we have tried to make sure that if you decide to buy bullion, you know the best possible way to do it rather than the most common. In the gold market, those two things are not always the same.

CHAPTER 6

Technical Analysis

The gold market doesn't trend the way the stock market does. In fact, the currency market in general trends differently than other major financial markets do because it tends to be "mean reverting." The gold market is also different from stocks because it is not designed to provide a return, and that neutrality affects the price action. From the government's perspective it would be ideal to have very small currency fluctuations against gold or other major currencies. There were many attempts to fix forex or gold rates within a narrow channel in the past, but they were not successful in the long term. As a result, free-floating currencies (including gold) tend to have trends that can be fairly long-lasting in both directions. Because gold is a currency, the only way one would expect it to trend upward indefinitely is if all other currencies moved to zero, which does not seem likely.

Understanding the difference between the gold (currency) market and the stock market is important because many of the assumptions you have as a stock trader do not apply to gold. One of the difficult things to do as you adjust your analytical models will be to let go of positive or negative feelings about trends in the gold market. Unlike stocks, a downtrend in gold is not bad news, and similarly, an uptrend is not good news. If over the long term gold does begin to revert back to its mean value versus the U.S. dollar, you will need to stay flexible, and technical analysis can be a useful tool to understand these shorter trends in the market.

In this section of the book we will be digging into some technical analysis methodologies and tools that perform well in the gold market; that should give you enough detail to get going on your own analysis. We will be using some of these tools and methods later in the book when we cover specific long-term and short-term trading strategies. However, make sure that before you dig into technical analysis you have access to a good charting source. In this book we have used professional-grade charts from MetaStock, but there are other good resources you can use for free or for a very low cost. A little later in this section we will provide a few specific recommendations for charting tools you can start using today.

TECHNICAL INDICATORS

Technical indicators are very flexible, but like all analytical tools they are easy to misuse and can be meaningless to a novice analyst. Indicators are most effective when they are used to filter the noise in the market and usually are designed to summarize information visually so that it is a little easier to make an estimate about the future trend. They also can be used to time an entry or exit in the market on a short-term basis.

Most technical indicators use one or more of three data components—price, volume, and time—to produce a graph that is displayed on, above, or below the gold price chart. Technical indicators are parameterized, which means they can be easily modified and adjusted to suit your preferences and strategies. Although there are hundreds of different indicators available, they tend to fall into two or three primary categories.

Moving Averages and Price Bands

This category includes studies as simple as a moving average based on the average of gold's closing price over a specified look-back period or as complicated as volatility bands that expand or contract around the charted price on the basis of volatility and direction. The look-back period for these indicators varies from trader to trader, but common parameters include 30-, 50-, and 200-period moving averages.

Oscillators

This is a category of technical indicators that we get a lot of questions about because they can be modified in several different ways and overoptimized to match historical prices. There are also a lot of "advisors" in the market who will sell a particular oscillator or formula that isn't that different from other versions that have been used for decades. Because no methodology or indicator will be right all the time, we generally opt for consistency and use a few of the most common indicators with the original definitions and parameters. Oscillators usually are designed to show the strength of the underlying trend, which is useful for short-term traders looking for a timing signal.

Volatility or Sentiment Indicators

These indicators lag prices the least and are very difficult to overoptimize, which means that the data from volatility indicators are more standard and easier to compare from one analyst to the next. The most important sentiment indicator we will cover is the CBOE Volatility Index (VIX), which has been used by stock and options traders for decades. That may sound funny to a gold trader, but gold and stock prices are often very sensitive to the same underlying changes in investor fear and confidence.

Like price patterns and Fibonacci analysis, technical indicators are time-frame-independent, which means that they should work just as well on a 10-minute or hourly charts as they do on daily or weekly charts; however, that is true only in theory. The problem is that trading costs are much higher in shorter time frames, and unless you can develop some kind of special edge (not very likely), short-term trading will be very difficult.

In general, we both consider ourselves to be primarily technical analysts or "chartists," which means that we believe charting is the most effective way to analyze fundamental data, trader sentiment, capital flow, and risk; however, we are acutely aware of the traps new analysts fall into when they start using indicators and price charts. These problems are important to understand before you begin using technical analysis to make a decision about a trade.

Indicator Piling

Indicator piling is our term for the practice of adding a larger number of technical indicators to a chart in an effort to increase the odds of a successful outcome. This is a very common problem for new technical analysts and is particularly pronounced among new traders in the gold and currency markets. For example, imagine that after some experience you find that 40 percent of the trades you have taken based on the Moving Average Convergence-Divergence (MACD), an oscillator, are profitable and 30 percent of the trades you have taken based on a moving average have been winners. It might be tempting to assume that if you wait until these two indicators agree, your winning percentage will go up because you are being more selective and waiting for a "double check" from the second indicator. We have seen many new traders attempt this with expectations that combining the two indicators will increase their winning ratio to 70 percent, which is the sum of both probabilities.

It doesn't take long to figure out that the winning percentage will not rise with the addition of more indicators and in fact often will be worse than it is with either of the two methodologies used alone. The problem is that even if we assume that technical indicators give you a probability of a successful outcome (they don't, and we will explain why later), they can't be used together because the analysis is being conducted with replacement. This is a statistician's way of saying that because the indicators cannot affect each other, adding more of them to a chart will not increase the probability of a successful outcome. Theoretically, the probability of a successful outcome when piling on more indicators should not be greater than that of the least accurate indicator because you must wait for agreement among all the indicators you are using, including the weakest.

The reason chances for finding winners probably have declined below the performance of the least effective indicator is that you are increasing the amount of lag when you are entering a trade, which causes you to miss a large percentage of the possible gains in the trend. This also adds to the amount of lag before you exit a trade, causing you to be in the market longer than you might have been after a trade has started to go bad. The underlying message here is a positive one. Managing a crowded chart and waiting for dozens of indicators to agree is time-consuming and confusing. Specializing and becoming proficient in a simplified analysis does have advantages. Keep in mind that technical and fundamental analyses are only tools that we use to try to predict the future, which will never be an exact science.

Overfitting

Because technical indicator parameters can be modified and adjusted in an infinite number of ways, traders often fall into the trap of overfitting an indicator to look good on the basis of past data. That means that the trader has changed the common parameters of a particular indicator and adjusted them until the indicator matches past price performance perfectly; however, because price movement in the gold market is not normally distributed (too many large outliers), this kind of overfitting to past price data will not improve the odds that it will continue performing in the future.

There is a lot of debate about what parameters work best for a specific technical indicator, but we usually suggest opting for the most common parameters, which are usually the original parameters defined by an indicator's creator. If you are interested in digging into more of the details behind the most popular technical indicators and how they were created, we recommend books by John Bollinger, Welles Wilder, and Gerald Appel, the creators of Bollinger bands, the RSI oscillator, and the MACD, respectively.

USING INDICATORS TO IDENTIFY TRENDS

Technical indicators tend to fall into one of three categories, but each of those categories can be used to identify trend direction and/or the strength of a trend, which is very important to gold traders. By its nature, gold is sentiment-driven, which means its trends can be fast and dramatic, and so understanding what the trend is helps with proper trade setups and modifications. The trend is a simple concept when you are looking at past data, but in the heat of the trade it can be much more difficult to decide whether the trend you are trading is intact or has reversed.

The chief marketing officer of a large currency and gold dealer told us several years ago that if retail traders could learn to trade trends and avoid channels, they would be much more successful. That is true, but if you knew when the trend was going to start and when it would end, you could become independently wealthy overnight. He was frustrated that traders couldn't grasp this seemingly simple concept; but of course, like many C-level brokerage managers, he wasn't a trader and didn't realize he was asking for nothing less than the Holy Grail of technical analysis. Being able to tell the difference between a continuing trend and an emerging channel or trend reversal is incredibly difficult in the moment; however, there are a few things we can do to make it a little easier on ourselves with technical indicators.

In the next example, we will use two technical indicators to identify the existing trend, which will define our trade direction, and spot potential breakout points, which will define the trade timing.

Is the Long-Term Trend Positive or Negative?

Moving averages are simple to use and can be effective trend indicators when two are used together. Although there are an unlimited number of combinations, a standard trend indicator like this consists of a 50-period and a 200-period moving average (MA). The trend is identified as positive when the 50-period MA is above the 200-period MA, and the reverse is true for a downtrend. You can see an example of gold prices with a 50- and a 200-period moving average creating a "golden cross" (A) and identifying an uptrend through 2009 in Figure 6-1.

In the financial press you often hear a cross of the 50-MA below the 200-MA described as a death cross and a cross of the 50-MA above the 200-MA referred to as a golden cross. These are dramatic terms and probably overplay their real significance, but it does help illustrate that the gold trading community keeps an eye on these indicators as an important trend indicator.

Is Gold Ready for a Breakout?

This is where technicians start to fine-tune the entry signal in favor of the prevailing bull trend. Gold prices are delicate, and because it is a highly leveraged market, investors tend to respond very quickly to news or other unexpected events. The result is that when gold prices get quiet or begin moving in a narrow range, the odds of a breakout start to rise. An easy way to tell that prices are channeling narrowly before a potential breakout is to apply a Bollinger band technical indicator. This tool consists of a short-term moving average and two bands that are placed two standard deviations above and below the short-term moving average. In English this means

FIGURE 6-1

Spot gold prices with 50- and 200-period moving averages,
January 2009–June 2010.

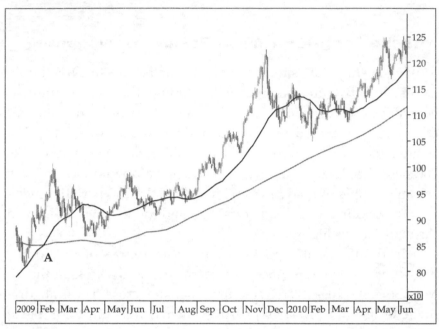

Source: MetaStock

that the indicator looks like two lines above and below gold's price
that will narrow, or "squeeze," when prices are too quiet and
widen very quickly when volatility picks back up.

Figure 6-2 shows a series of squeezes that occurred during
August (A), September (B), and October (C) 2009. Each squeeze
occurred at a logical level of support (a prior high) and predicted
a breakout to the upside. This is a classic trend-based entry signal
in which traders would have been buying new long positions
after the squeeze breakouts because the 50- and 200-period moving averages were already indicating that the prevailing trend
was bullish.

Most traders will preempt the actual support bounce and
make the trade when the squeeze is beginning to tighten as the

FIGURE 6-2

Spot gold prices with Bollinger bands, January 2009–June 2010.

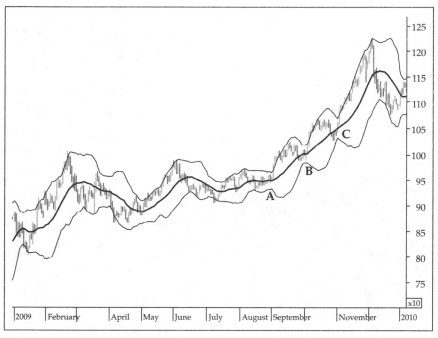

Source: MetaStock

market hits support but before prices have started to make a move. In Figure 6-3 you can see a close-up example of the squeeze that occurred on October 28, 2010, when prices retraced to support of $1,026 (equal to the prior high in September) and then moved nearly 20 percent over the next month before topping out at the beginning of December.

Making a trade under these conditions will not result in 100 percent winners, so if you have never been a short-term trader before, practice before you put real money at risk. Even longer-term traders who are using a trend-based technical signal like this for new entries or additions to an existing long position should practice with the tools before they start making trades with real money.

FIGURE 6-3

Spot gold prices with Bollinger bands, October
2009–December 2009

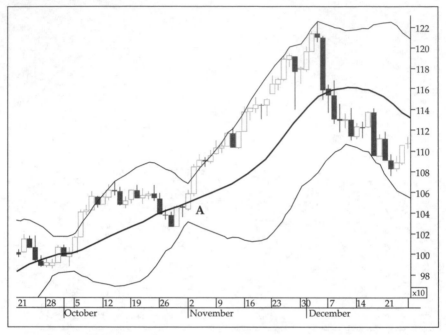

Source: MetaStock

Fortunately, trending indicators are by far the most common
technical tools in the market, and just about every charting package includes them. They are easy to apply to the chart and provide
a clear estimate of the trend and sometimes the potential for a new
breakout. Traders can't predict when the trend will reverse or
when a whipsaw (a quick back-and-forth move in gold's price) will
wipe out some recent gains with perfect accuracy, but most analysts agree that trading with the trend helps provide a small edge
for traders willing to take risks. In the strategies section of the book
we will use trending indicators in a real-life example of setting up
for an intermediate-term trade.

WHY "OVERBOUGHT" AND "OVERSOLD" DON'T MEAN WHAT YOU THINK

Oscillators are often erroneously classified as reversal indicators; most are actually much better at identifying the trend than at signaling reversals. We tend to shy away from oscillators because they lag prices so much; however, they are used by institutional-level traders quite a bit and can be useful in the right circumstances. Unlike trending indicators, oscillators usually are applied above or below the price chart in a subwindow. Figure 6-4 shows an oscillator, the Commodity Channel Index (CCI), applied to gold prices in 2009. When the CCI shows a reading above 100, the market is considered overbought (point A in September 2009), and a reading

FIGURE 6-4

Spot gold prices with the CCI technical indicator, January 2009–December 2009.

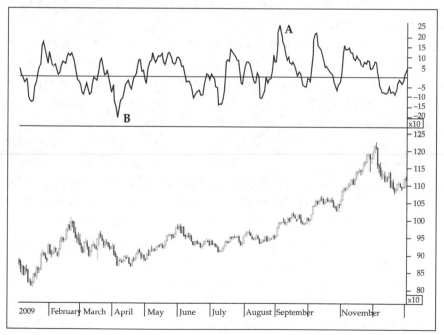

Source: MetaStock

below –100 (point B in April 2009) is considered oversold. If you look closely at the chart, you will notice that the CCI was over-bought much more than it was oversold during 2009, which is expected during an uptrend.

The terms "overbought" and "oversold" are a little mislead-ing in the gold market because that market can trend for so long. Oversold does not automatically mean traders should buy in at bargain prices, and overbought does not mean that gold is over-priced and bulls should stay out. The readings are more valuable when viewed within the context of the trend. If the gold market is generally bullish, the CCI can stay in overbought territory for an extended period, and a reading like that is a strong signal that new long positions look good. During a bull market the brief oversold readings can be used for new buy signals, but if gold is in a bear market, short-term long positions probably should be avoided.

Like Bollinger bands and moving averages, the CCI can create very powerful signals when gold prices are sitting at support in an uptrend or resistance in a downtrend. Figure 6-5 shows each time the CCI signaled oversold conditions when prices were also in an uptrend and the subsequent rally after the technical signal. When used like this, an oscillator won't produce very many entry signals during a trend, but for an investor attempting to optimize her long-term positions or adjustments, it should work well.

A common mistake that gold traders make is to use oversold or overbought readings as a signal to stop and reverse a trade. Because the market is volatile and oscillators can move very quick-ly between two extremes, trading in and out of the market in that manner will lead to losses. The first issue with this strategy is that technical indicators lag prices because they rely on a look-back period such as a moving average. This means that when gold prices move suddenly, the indicator follows later; that is fine if you are using an oscillator to time your entry in favor of the existing trend, but it also will lead to early exits and countertrend positions that are much more risky. The second problem is that "stop-and-

FIGURE 6-5

Spot gold prices with oversold CCI readings, March
2009–November 2009.

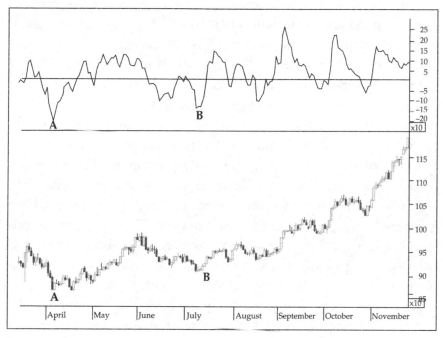

Source: MetaStock

reverse" systems suffer from overtrading during channels, and that
will drive up trading costs.

Using the oscillator within the context of the trend will help
improve your results, but inevitably there will be bad trades and
investments. No oscillator can pinpoint an accurate entry every
time, and this should tell you something about how much time to
spend on analysis versus the other parts of the trading process.
Successful gold traders tend to obey the Pareto principle (the 80–20
rule) when it comes to investing and spend much more of their
time working on the factors they can control, including position
sizing, money management, diversification, and cost reduction.

FINDING REVERSALS WITH DIVERGENCES

This may just be personal preference, but in general we find that technical indicators are like training wheels for new investors and don't provide any information one couldn't get by observing the price action itself. However, there is an exception to this rule: Oscillators do a great job of warning about trend reversals. Trend reversal signals are important because they are a warning that a disruption is likely. In a bull market, a reversal signal isn't the trigger to sell your long positions and short the market immediately, but it is a good timing signal for the right moment to tighten your risk control and evaluate any outstanding positions. The inverse is true during a bearish trend. Reversal signals are not helpful only for trade management within a trend; smaller reversal signals are great trade entry points in favor of the prevailing long-term trend.

Because oscillators smooth prices over a look-back period, the way a moving average does, they won't show some of the extreme prices that will appear in the actual price chart, which in this case is an advantage. A divergence is signaled when the extreme peaks and valleys of a price chart do not match the direction of the peaks and valleys on the oscillator. These divergences happen during bullish and bearish trends alike, and in the gold market they are equally productive.

Bearish Divergence

Figure 6-6 shows how two sequentially higher highs in gold prices were not matched by the peaks on the MACD oscillator applied to the chart. The MACD actually showed lower highs, indicating a potential break in the trend. This was happening in the middle of a robust uptrend in the gold market in 2010, and so we wouldn't consider it an exit signal in May through June, but it was a great time to apply a little extra risk control (such as selling a covered call) to an existing long position. The subsequent correction through the

FIGURE 6-6

Spot gold prices with a bearish MACD divergence,
September 2009–August 2010.

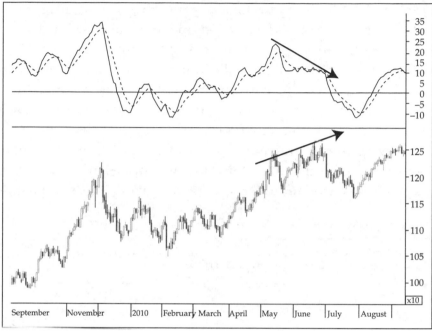

Source: MetaStock

month of July was 8 percent, so having a little extra protection or
diversification during that period would have been very helpful
for gold traders who were feeling the squeeze.

Bullish Divergence

A bullish divergence is the mirror image of the bearish version, and
because gold has been in a long-term uptrend, we tend to pay more
attention to these signals than to the former. If the Fed ever restores
confidence and raises interest rates and the U.S. dollar keeps its
dominance as the world's reserve currency (try to hold in your
laughter), that bias may change. A bullish divergence is helpful in
a long-term uptrend as a trigger to buy into the market.

Figure 6-7 shows how a bullish MACD divergence in the short-term charts (in this case a two-hour period) led to a very nice rally in gold prices for the next two weeks. The divergence completed on October 22, 2010, and by the time a bearish divergence emerged on November 9, 2010, prices had moved up $60 an ounce and had been up as much as $90 an ounce at the peak of that short-term trend. We use a short-term chart here to illustrate how technical analysis is time-frame-independent; it doesn't matter what time frame you use for your charting periods as long as you remain consistent and understand that shorter-term trading will lead to higher costs.

Divergences like this are easy to find and simple to use in your trading. We used the MACD in this case because it does a very good job at smoothing erroneous price spikes. A faster-moving

FIGURE 6-7

Spot gold prices with a bearish MACD divergence, September 2009–August 2010.

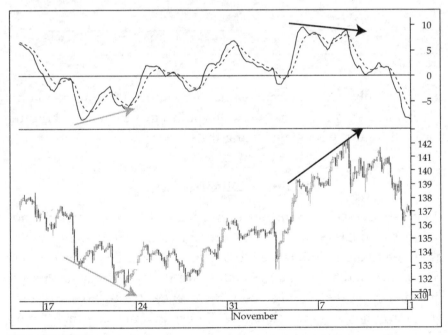

Source: MetaStock

oscillator such as the CCI would be too responsive and not as good at finding those moments when prices are most likely to be overextended. You will get more signals from a faster-moving oscillator, but more of them will be false alarms. This is one situation in which the lag works in our favor and can produce very effective trading signals in the gold market.

THE VIX

The Chicago Board Options Exchange (CBOE) produces the Volatility Index (VIX), which is available in most charting programs. The VIX is not a stock or an option; it is an index that measures stock investor sentiment. That may not sound very useful to gold traders, but it is actually very helpful because gold and stocks compete for investment dollars. If the VIX can tell us how traders feel about stocks, it can also tell us a lot about the demand for gold. Sometimes traders refer to the VIX as the "fear index" because it rises when investor fear is rising and confidence is low. The VIX does this by measuring the implied volatility levels of the S&P 500 index options, which will rise when investors are worried about a decline in stocks. For example, in Figure 6-8 you can see how high the VIX rose when investors reacted to the collapse of Lehman Brothers in September 2008 and the stock market really started to fall.

By the time the VIX broke resistance and started reaching all-time highs in early October 2008, most investors knew we were in for something very unusual. The rest of the story is well known: Stocks crashed, and gold has rallied almost 100 percent in price. This short example should tell you something about why the VIX is an indicator to which gold traders pay attention. Fear and confidence play a major role in gold prices; therefore, if investors are fearful, they will seek safety, and after the U.S. dollar, gold is second on the list of safe-haven investments. We expect that the U.S. dollar's role as the premier short-term shelter against market panics will end in the next few years and gold will take its place permanently; that means that

FIGURE 6-8

The CBOE Volatility Index before and after the September
2008 Lehman Brothers collapse, January 2008–December
2008.

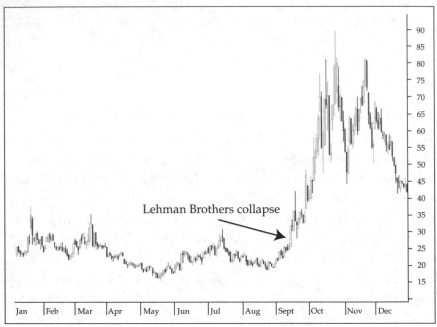

Source: MetaStock

when fear rises to extraordinary levels, traders will increase their long bias toward gold.

It doesn't take a full market panic to see the relationship between the VIX and gold prices; for example, in Figure 6-9 the VIX indicated that investor fear began to accelerate in May 2010. This wasn't a true panic, but it did lead to a large decline in stock prices. Gold followed the VIX (and investor fear) all the way up and then trailed the VIX all the way down later that summer. Later in 2010 gold prices rallied to new highs after the VIX spiked in early August. The correlation between the rise in gold prices and the VIX seems remarkable until you think about the underlying fundamental that drives both: fear. When fear spikes but remains rela-

FIGURE 6-9

The CBOE Volatility Index versus spot gold prices (solid line), March 2010–July 2010.

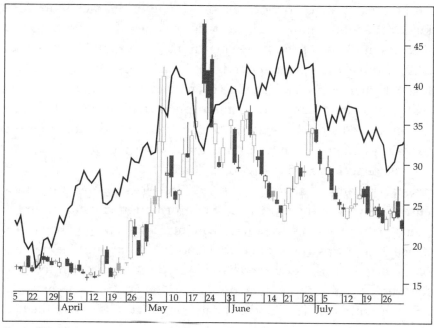

Source: MetaStock

tively under control, gold will be very responsive and is also likely to rise. When fear spikes into panic territory, we expect gold to be a little choppy, but it should still win over the long term.

If gold prices spike during a burst of investor fear, what do you suppose happens when confidence is restored (however temporarily) and the VIX drops? If everything else is equal, a decline in fear should be bad for gold prices; however, recent market conditions have been such that a confident market is also very bearish on the zero-yielding dollar, and that tends to be supportive for gold. If market conditions change in the future (higher rates, better growth, low inflation, etc.), we might expect gold to follow the VIX lower, but to us such a change seems unlikely, so for now we recommend using the VIX solely to time a new or larger entry into a bullish gold position.

INTRODUCTION TO FIBONACCI ANALYSIS

Technical analysts look at past price action to make an estimate about future price changes. Besides the trend, one of the most important kinds of past price movement are cycles: a series of interruptions and then resumptions of the prevailing trend. For example, since mid-2001 gold has been in an uptrend, but it hasn't risen in an unbroken line of higher prices; the trend has been interrupted many times over that period, and some of those interruptions have been very regular and even predictive. Fibonacci analysis is the method technicians use to make estimates about the future from those past cycles.

Fibonacci analysis is used to forecast levels of support and resistance, project price targets, set stop-losses, and time new entries; however, the most valuable information is what it can tell you about risk. In this section we will introduce a few of the tactical concepts and tips you will need to understand about this method-ology before using it on the charts. As you read through the next few sections, take some time to replicate the analysis on your own charting software. This kind of hands-on practice is one of the best ways to make sure you understand how to use the tools effectively.

As a mathematical phenomenon, Fibonacci analysis has been around for thousands of years, and it is still used to study and model biological growth rates, architectural design, financial mar-kets, and even computer search algorithms. The analysis is based on the Fibonacci number series popularized by a thirteenth-centu-ry mathematician named Leonardo Fibonacci but was well known in India a thousand years before that. The technical tools that are applied to price charts that rely on the Fibonacci number series include retracements, projections, and fan lines.

A Few Issues

The problem with both fundamental and technical analysis is that both are very subjective, which means that they allow for a great deal of interpretation and individual preference. New traders would love to learn a few rules that are simple to memorize and can be applied to the market without the need to make any qualitative judgments. That feeling is completely understandable, but unfortunately, the market is inherently ambiguous and there is a healthy debate among analysts about the best or most proper way to use a particular fundamental or charting tool. In this section, we will give you some details about what is debated most about Fibonacci analysis and the way you should deal with some of that ambiguity.

Where Is the Trend?

If you are analyzing a trend, how can you be sure you have identified the real top or bottom, not just a temporary countertrend move? To a certain extent this question is unanswerable, but through the case studies in this section you will learn a few basic guidelines that should help. Keep in mind that the real key is to remain flexible and be willing to adjust your analysis when it becomes clear that market conditions are changing.

Bodies or Shadows?

There is a minor debate among technicians about whether you should base Fibonacci studies and trend lines on the body of a price candlestick (the fat part of a candlestick) or the shadows (the skinny vertical lines above and below the bodies). We think that the shadows should be included because they represent the extremes of market sentiment during a candlestick's period.

Support and Resistance Lines or Areas?

Support and resistance is more of a wide band around the Fibonacci lines than a specific to-the-penny point on a price chart. You will find that prices move around a support or resistance line quite a bit, and ignoring that level because of a temporary break may lead you to ignore a valid signal.

Charting Studies

As with most technical indicators, there are several different Fibonacci tools to choose from, and the parameters can be adjusted in many ways. We will be using the most common Fibonacci tools, including retracements, targets, fan lines, and time studies.

Charting Software

Fibonacci tools used to be included only in professional-level charting software, but as smaller traders have become more independent, those tools have been making their way into more of the low-cost charting packages. If you are working with a broker who specializes in active traders, there is a good chance you will have Fibonacci tools in the charts in your trading software, but if you don't, we have included a few suggestions for charting packages that offer them for free or at a very low cost.

MetaStock

This Reuters product is an excellent charting package that is available for a low monthly subscription. It can't be matched for functionality and customizability, and you can try the product for 30 days for free at www.equis.com. This is the charting package we have used professionally for years and is the source of many of the chart illustrations in this book.

thinkorswim

This is actually a stock and options broker, but a few years ago it was acquired by the same company that produced the popular

Prophet.net charts. These are by far the easiest charts to learn and use if you are just starting out but want to have access to a robust tool set. Although the charting package is free, it requires a brokerage account. You can sign up for a paper trade account for free and check it out for yourself for a limited time. thinkorswim also offers world-class option analytical tools that would require a very large monthly subscription if you wanted to access them without a brokerage account. You can check these guys out at www.thinkorswim.com.[1]

FreeStockCharts.com

These charts may be free, but they are very robust. They can be accessed online only and were created by Worden Brothers, who have been in the charting software business for decades. The only drawback of these charts is that they cover only stocks, which isn't a problem if you are trading gold ETFs or gold stocks; however, if you want futures, you will have to look elsewhere.

What Is a Fibonacci Ratio?

This kind of analysis is based on the Fibonacci ratios, which are 23.6 percent, 38.2 percent, 61.8 percent, and 161.8 percent and represent the distance between sequential numbers in the Fibonacci series. The Fibonacci number series is created by starting at 0 and 1 and then adding the two previous numbers to arrive at the next number in the series. For example, if you start at 0, 1 and add those two numbers together, you get another 1, then a 2, then a 3, and so forth. If you carry out that addition for 15 iterations, you will get a number series like this: 0, 1, 1, 2, 3, 5, 8, 13, 21, 34, 55, 89, 144, 233, 377.

The Fibonacci ratios are based on the quotient of the difference between two sequential numbers in the series divided by one

---

[1] Full disclosure: Wade Hansen and John Jagerson both worked for thinkorswim Group, Inc., until 2007.

of those two numbers. You can see an example of what that means below by pulling out three sequential numbers (21, 34, 55) from the series and analyzing the difference between them. The ratios that appear in the example following are the ones we will use in the chart studies later in this section.

$$(34 - 21)/34 = 38.2 \text{ percent}$$
$$(34 - 21)/55 = 23.6 \text{ percent}$$
$$(34 - 21)/21 = 61.8 \text{ percent}$$

There are also very important Fibonacci ratios that we use to create price projections within a trend after a breakout. Projection ratios are based on the quotient of two sequential numbers in the Fibonacci series. For example, using the same three numbers above (21, 34, and 55), you can see how these projection ratios are calculated.

$$34/21 = 161.8 \text{ percent}$$
$$55/21 = 261.8 \text{ percent}$$

The ratio 61.8 percent is particularly important to traders and is often referred to as phi, or the golden ratio. This ratio has been used to determine ideal proportions in architecture and art for millennia because designs based on it (including the human face and body) are very pleasing to the eye. Artists, graphic designers, photographers, and even the ancient Greeks have used the golden ratio to develop history's most well-known designs. For example, the Parthenon is based on the golden ratio along its width, height, and depth; the average distance from a person's navel to the top of that person's head compared with the average distance from the navel to the bottom of the feet is also the golden ratio. How closely the proportions of facial features conform to the golden ratio has a profound positive correlation with how beautiful a person is considered. No one knows why these ratios appear so often in nature, design, engineering, and the financial markets, but they work very well and can help you develop better profit targets and trading estimates.

Fibonacci Retracements

Fibonacci retracements work best when used in favor of the prior trend; that means that when you use a Fibonacci retracement to time your entry into a new long position, you will be more accurate if the longer-term trend is already heading up. A Fibonacci retracement study is better at finding support during a bull market and resistance levels in a bear market. It can be very tempting to be a contrarian and use technical tools such as Fibonacci retracements to short the top of the market or to buy at the bottom, but that kind of trading is very risky and difficult.

Fibonacci retracements, like all technical analysis, is considered time-frame-independent; therefore, the technical tool should be just as useful on the daily or weekly charts as it is on five-minute candlestick charts. In theory that is true, but in practice the costs of trading very short-term charts erode most of the edge you may get from the analysis. In the book we will use Fibonacci retracements on the daily charts; however, you should experiment to see how they work for you in the time frame in which you typically trade.

Figure 6-10 shows a Fibonacci retracement applied against the rally in gold prices that took place from July 28, 2010, through October 14, 2010. There are four major Fibonacci retracement levels drawn horizontally at different percentages through the trend, and each one represents a likely level of support and a potential entry point for a new long position. We have enhanced the study with a bold black right triangle that shows where the Fibonacci lines fall within the vertical distance of the trend. The vertical leg of the right triangle is bisected 23.6 percent, 38.2 percent, 50 percent, and 61.8 percent along its length starting from the top and moving toward the right angle at the bottom. The retracement lines show how far the market has moved (in actual dollar terms) against the trend.

Because gold was in a strong uptrend, the Fibonacci retracement lines helped identify areas of support where a trader could buy a new position; however, because each of the retracement lines

F I G U R E 6-10

Spot gold prices with Fibonacci retracement study, May 2010–October 2010.

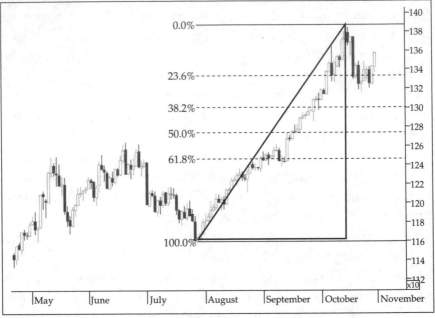

Source: MetaStock

is a candidate level of support, it is probably best to buy in after prices have bounced and begun to move back up. In this example, gold stopped at the 23.6 percent retracement level on October 19, which worked out to be a good reentry opportunity for buyers in the short term. You should continue to move the anchor points of the Fibonacci retracement as the market creates new highs. Figure 6-11 moves forward a little after the October bounce had established a new peak in November, and subsequently the market bounced again on the 38.2 percent Fibonacci retracement level.

You should notice how Fibonacci retracement levels tend to line up with each other over time; this is something that happens in the gold market because the cycles of trend interruptions are fairly regular. This is very easy to see when one is looking at historical

FIGURE 6-11

Spot gold prices with Fibonacci retracement study, May 2010–December 2010.

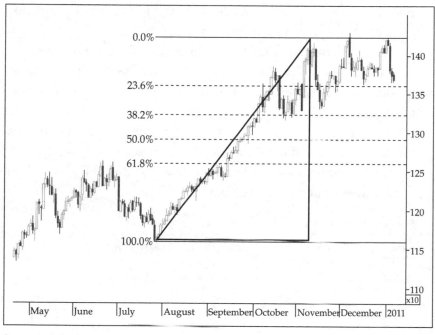

Source: MetaStock

charts, but in the heat of the moment it can be more challenging to make a decision while prices are moving and you are not sure whether support will hold. We highly recommend practicing your analysis by paper trading to develop a feel for the cycles in the gold market without having to worry about putting real money at risk.

Fibonacci Fans

A Fibonacci fan line is very similar to retracement levels and often is used to identify diagonal support or resistance levels in favor of the long-term trend. A fan line is based on the same right triangle that is used for a retracement study, but rather than being drawn horizontally through the vertical leg of the triangle, the fan lines are drawn at a slope by connecting the vertex of the triangle with its corresponding retracement level on the vertical leg. Figure 6-12 shows what this looks like when the fan lines are anchored to the trend we used in the last example. You will notice that the support bounce in November was identified by both studies.

Many technicians prefer fan lines to retracements because they tend to follow the trend rather than just bisecting it horizontally; this means that a fan line study does not need to be moved when the market makes higher highs in favor of the prevailing trend as long as prices stay within the fan line's range. We recommend that fan lines and retracements be used together, and at the end of this section you will see how this works and why it can help confirm a potential level of support.

FIGURE 6-12

Spot gold prices with Fibonacci fan lines, May 2010–December 2010.

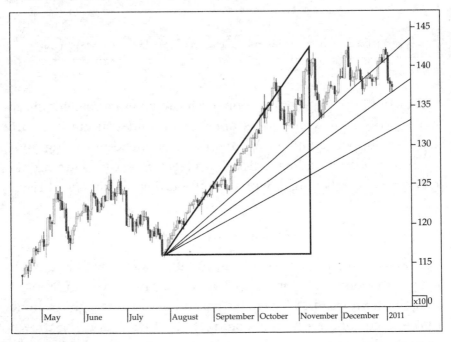

Source: MetaStock

Although fan lines have many advantages, they also have a couple of disadvantages. When the trend is very steep or the market channels for an extended period, they become useless because the market quickly moves outside the fan line's range. For example, in Figure 6-13 you can see what happened when a fan line study was applied to the very fast rally in gold prices that occurred from October 29, 2009, to December 3, 2009. In that case, the trend was so steep and fast that the fan lines just point straight up into the white space of the chart.

Fan lines can be very useful when they are combined with retracements; they often "agree" or cross each other at significant levels of support or resistance. Figure 6-14 shows the time period used in the last section on retracements; however, we have applied

FIGURE 6-13

Spot gold prices with Fibonacci fan lines, October 2009–June 2010

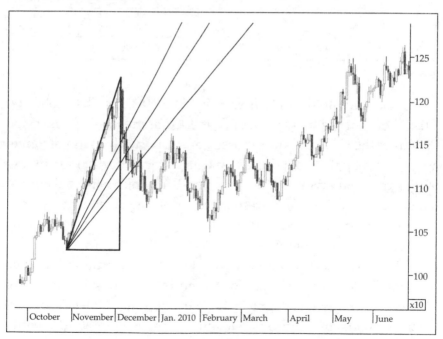

Source: MetaStock

Spot gold prices with Fibonacci fan lines and retracements,
May 2010–December 2010

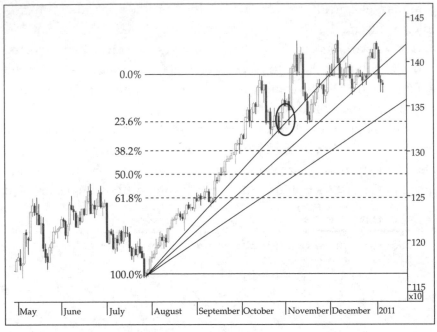

Source: MetaStock

a fan line study to the rally from July 28, 2010, through October 14, 2010. You can see that the bounce in October really happened the day after the two indicators crossed at support. This kind of agreement will happen periodically, and it is very effective for timing major rallies in favor of a prior uptrend. The opposite is also true: Fan studies will identify resistance levels most effectively in a longer-term downtrend and can be combined with retracements the way we did in this chart.

The gold market can be psychologically frustrating for some traders. There is a real temptation to short what looks like the top of the market or buy what appears to be the bottom of the trend; however, the odds are very much against your being able to identify major tops and bottoms. The beauty of Fibonacci retracements and fan lines is that they can ease this problem because they are designed to help you find new opportunities in favor of the long-term trend after the market has cooled off a little. Buying a support bounce in an uptrend or shorting a resistance bounce in a downtrend is less stressful than buying or shorting at a new high and low.

Creating Price Targets

Fibonacci retracement levels are particularly useful for making estimates about how far a support or resistance bounce may go in the near term. Making price target estimates is helpful in gold trading because it will help you evaluate whether the risk you are taking has the potential to be worth the reward. A projection level is created by applying a Fibonacci retracement study to the short countertrend move or interruption rather than the prior trend. When it is used like this, you aren't concerned with the horizontal levels within the triangle; instead, you will be using the projection levels outside the triangle.

A projection level is based on the horizontal leg of the right triangle used to draw retracement or fan lines; however, the projection level will appear above the right angle vertex of the triangle in an uptrend or below the right angle vertex in a downtrend. The most common projection levels are 161.8 percent and 261.8 percent, and they represent a lower and upper price target estimate. In Figure 6-15 you can see what this looks like with a projection that has been drawn from the start of the countertrend move on June 28, 2010, to the start of the rally on July 28, 2010, which is the same point we used to start the fan line and retracement study in the last two sections.

When you are using Fibonacci projection levels, you are not interested in the countertrend move but in where the market is targeted to move once it bounces off support. You can see in Figure 6-15 that the 161.8 percent retracement level at $1,330 was reached quickly and then acted as support (a very common situation), after

FIGURE 6-15

Spot gold prices with Fibonacci projection lines, April
2010–December 2010.

Source: MetaStock

which prices got within $4 an ounce of the second projection level
at $1,434, which has since acted as resistance. You should also
notice that these two common projection levels are versions of phi,
or the golden ratio.

Projection levels tell you where prices should go after a support bounce before a consolidation or another interruption in the
trend appears. Short-term traders may sell long positions at these
levels, and a long-term trader might evaluate a small modification
(such as a covered call or protective put) to reduce his risk a little
while preserving profits. The usefulness of a projection level does
not end once the price level is reached, because it is quite likely that
the market will move back to the same levels and treat them as support. In Figure 6-15 you can see how prices reached the 161.8 percent

projection level on October 5, 2010, and then returned to it as support later in October and November. Each of these support bounces was a new buy opportunity.

As you can imagine, we used a nice case study for the book so that the points we were trying to make would be very clear. In the real market there is no analytical methodology that will work all the time; therefore, as you apply this kind of analysis in your own trading, think about how you will respond to trades that do not conform to your original forecast. If you stay flexible, apply diversification, and position your trades appropriately, you will find that it is much easier to be patient when the market is getting a little choppy. Trading in and out of a gold ETF or futures contract every time prices nudge their way slightly outside a particular support or resistance line is a great way to drive up costs in your account and revenue for your broker.

CHAPTER 7

Long-Term Investing

Investors considering gold as a component of a diversified long-term portfolio have to make two key decisions. The first is what kind of gold investment should be held, which is something we discussed in the good products section of the book; the second is how much of the portfolio should be held in gold. Should it be a 20/30/50 percent split between gold, bonds, and equities, respectively, or the other way around? There are no hard and fast rules that can be used to answer the second question because your gold allocation will depend on your tolerance for risk, personal interests, and expectations for the future. However, we suggest that whatever you decide, the gold allocation should be substantial.

However, gold investors should beware of becoming overweight in gold, which would defeat the benefits of diversification. Because gold is a nonyielding asset that is not designed to rise in price, its primary purpose as part of your portfolio is to reduce overall account volatility. Lowering volatility is a very big deal over the long term because it can make the difference between achieving your investing objectives within the time frame you have planned and never making your goals.

Table 7-1 illustrates the point with a comparison of six different investors, five of whom have a concentrated portfolio and one
of whom has an evenly diversified group of assets that are rebal-
anced annually. The returns shown are based on indexed Vanguard
funds and gold spot prices over a 16-year period.

So far it would seem that each strategy did pretty well. The
real estate investor did the best, but there is no way anyone could
have foreseen the amazing real estate bull market that lasted
through 2007. There are probably a lot of traders who would be
surprised that the two assets that are purportedly the best hedges
against inflation (gold and stocks) were nearly tied for last place.
The second runner-up was the diversified investor, which is pretty
much what we should expect in a comparison like this, and on the
surface most investors would be happy with the returns of just
about any of these asset classes, but that's because we have the benefit of hindsight. Those 16 years had some pretty dramatic ups and
downs, which you can see in Figure 7-1, where we have graphed
the hypothetical returns of a $10,000 investment over this 16-year
period to get a feel for which investor really did the best on the
basis of overall account volatility.

Real estate may have come out on top in this example, but
when you look at the chart, would you have had the discipline to

TABLE 7-1

Returns from Various Investing Styles

Investing Style	Total Return 1995–2010, %
Large-cap stocks	+327
Gold bullion	+341
Investment-grade bonds	+344
Residential real estate	+550
Emerging markets	+361
Diversified evenly across all five asset classes	+464

FIGURE 7-1

Individual asset class returns versus diversified portfolio,
January 1995–December 2010.

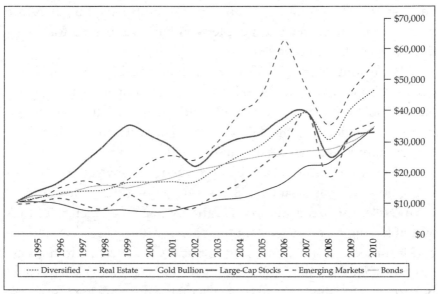

Source: Vanguard, Federal Reserve

withstand a 25 percent drawdown in both 2007 and 2008? Similarly, the large-cap stock returns we made in the first five years and have since been flat; would you have known that in advance and been able to avoid the big drawdowns after the dot-bomb crisis of 2001 and the liquidity freeze of 2008? Gold seems like a very compelling investment now, but for the first six years it went nowhere; would you have kept your investment? These are all subjective questions that have very subjective answers, but they are important. A diversified portfolio will keep your equity curve smooth and growing, which is a critical set of objectives for a long-term investor.

Being diversified is like admitting that you don't know which asset class will outperform in the future and which assets contain hidden risks that could be a portfolio killer. Admitting you have no idea what the future holds is the first step toward portfolio recovery. Investment books and Web sites that advocate 100 percent allocation into gold (there are many) may seem pretty smart right now because they have the benefit of survivorship bias, but there are many more gurus and salespeople who have advocated for a particular asset class and have been wrong.

For example, there was a very interesting book released this decade about why you should buy gold to protect against a collapsing dollar. It has sold very well, and as it turns out, gold did go up in value (a lot) and the dollar declined after its publication. That is very impressive market timing—or is it?

One of the authors has been producing a newsletter advocating gold ownership since 1987. Along with other current gold gurus/celebrities, this author is arguably just a beneficiary of luck and of having a very consistent message for the last 23 years. In the end it turned out that he was right, but it took 20 years to happen. The problem with hard-line positions that advocate a single-asset portfolio is that they tend to be very volatile over the long term. We advocate managing your portfolio by underestimating your ability to predict the future rather than overestimating it. That will keep you safer and less concentrated in the long term.

We have two points to make in this section. First, gold as part of a long-term diversified portfolio makes sense because it lowers account volatility. Gold is not an asset that we expect to appreciate in value like stocks or to create income like bonds. Its real value for a long-term investor is portfolio insurance against risks that are serious but very hard to predict. The market crashes of 2001 and 2008–2010 are great examples of why investors should have a gold allocation in their portfolios.

The second point is that there is a lot of hype and many conflicts of interest in the gold investing world. Many gold gurus or analysts know a lot about gold and economics but may not be very forthcoming about their track record of predicting the future. Gold investors looked pretty smart in 2010 but not so smart 20 years earlier; therefore, you need to be able to make your own decision about whether you will hold gold and how much.

COVERED CALLS

Long-term investing is all about being diversified and keeping costs low. That usually means that you are buying investments that can be held with minimal fees and that represent many different asset classes. It shouldn't be very complicated or overoptimized because a simpler strategy is easier to maintain and execute. However, diversification can mean more than making sure you have a gold component mixed in with your stocks and bonds. Strategic diversification is one way to increase your performance over the long term without having to increase your efforts or costs substantially.

Strategic diversification is a broad subject, but one of the specific recommendations we regularly make to long-term investors is to start with something that builds on their existing positions. For example, covered call writing is used by small and large investors in the gold market to reduce account volatility and increase profitability over the long term without significantly increasing risk. Covered calls are executed by selling or writing a call with a short-term expiration against your gold holdings (usually an ETF or gold stock position) and then repeating the process each time the last call option expires.

Example of Writing a Covered Call

In this example we will assume that you are holding gold bullion ETF shares in your portfolio because they have very low fees, track gold prices very closely, and have extremely liquid options. Selling a single call option against your ETF position means that you are giving someone the right to buy 100 ETF shares (a single call contract represents 100 shares of stock) from you for the strike price before the expiration date. If the option expires out of the money, you get to keep the premium and the option expires worthless. If the option expires in the money, the stock will be "called" and you will get to keep the option premium and will be paid the strike price for the shares as if you had sold the stock.

For example, on December 20, 2010, the SPDR Gold Shares ETF (GLD) was priced at $135.11 per share and a January 2011 call option with a strike price of $136 was selling for $2.05 per share, or $205 per contract. Traders who wrote that covered call received the premium from the call up front. No matter what happened, as long as they held the stock through January's expiration, that premium was theirs to keep. A covered call premium is income that helps offset a loss in a bad month or makes a profit when prices are rising. In this case, by the time the January option expires, there are two possible outcomes.

Scenario 1: The Stock Rises, and the Option Is Called Out
Assume that GLD rose to $139 per share by expiration in January, which would result in the stock being called for $136 and a net profit of $2.94 per share ($2.05 option premium plus $0.89 profit in the stock). That sounds good but is actually less than what the profits would have been by holding the stock and not selling the call.

Scenario 2: The Stock Falls, and the Option Expires Worthless
Assume that GLD falls to $132 per share by expiration in January. The option buyer will not exercise the contract, and you will keep the premium and the stock. This has resulted in a net loss of $1.06 per share ($2.05 option premium minus $3.11 loss on the stock), which is much lower than the losses without the option premium.

This is a simple example that required no market timing, option analytics, or charting, which is exactly how this strategy should be implemented by a long-term trader. The key is to be consistent and not worry about the smaller profits during a bullish month because the smaller losses in a bad month are where you get an edge. Making back your losses is much more difficult than making gains because you have less money to work with; therefore, capital preservation is your first priority as a long-term investor, and call selling can create strategic diversification that increases your ability to protect your capital.

Because bullion-backed ETFs are relatively new (introduced in 2004 or later), we don't have long-term data to make a historical case for the value of selling covered calls against a long-term position. However, such studies do exist for stock indexes, and option pricing theory suggests that the same thing should be true for gold ETFs. A gold investor using the strategy of selling the first out-of-the-money call each month right after the last call has expired should expect three things.

1. You will underperform gold during a robust bull market because despite the call premium, your winners will be cut short in many months.

2. You will outperform gold during a bear market because your losing months will be partially offset by the call premium that you get to keep.

3. Over the long term (bull trends and bear trends), a consistent covered call seller will outperform other traders who held gold long, because the covered call seller had smaller losses during bear markets and made money in flat trends.

Practical Issues with Covered Calls

This is not a complicated strategy, but there are a few things to consider before implementing it in your portfolio. As usual, the devil is in the details, and you may have to make some changes in your account structure to use a strategy like this effectively.

Not All Brokers and Retirement Plan Administrators
Will Allow You to Sell Covered Calls

This is becoming less of an issue all the time as competition for clients increases, but if you aren't using a strategy like this right now, you may need to discuss it with your broker first to make sure you can. Don't worry if you need to make a change; there are plenty of great brokers who would love to help you start selling covered calls within your portfolio.

You Will Pay a Commission Each Time You
Sell a Covered Call or Have to Deal with Exercise

Not all brokers charge the same fees, and a little research can help you make sure you are not paying too much for the strategy. Make sure you consider the costs relative to the size of your account before implementing an active strategy like this because very small investors often find that commissions eat up a lot of their monthly premiums.

Should You Buy the Call Back before It Is Exercised or
Let It Get Exercised and Then Buy the Stock Back Later?

If the option is in the money at expiration, it probably will be called and the stock will be taken out of your account. Some traders will allow that to happen and then buy the stock back after expiration, and some prefer to buy the callback to close the trade right before expiration to avoid being called out. Either strategy is fine, but if you decide to buy the callback before expiration, you may be surprised once in a while with early exercise. This is rare, but it happens now and then when a call has moved deep in the money.

Some Traders Decide to Skip the Hassle of Owing the Stock and
Selling Covered Calls Each Month and Just Sell Naked Puts

When we mention this strategy to new traders, they get a little nervous because selling a naked put is very, very risky—right? Actually, if the put is cash-secured (this means that you have enough cash in your account to cover the cost of the stock if the put is exercised), the risk profile is identical to that of a covered call. The biggest difference is that if you are selling an out-of-the-money put, you have a little better risk protection if gold falls, but you also make a little less if gold rises.

PROTECTIVE PUTS

We have discussed the concept of a protective put several times in the book. Sometimes this term is used generically to describe any form of portfolio insurance or asset protection strategy, but it also refers to a specific option trade that long-term investors can use to reduce the risk of a significant drop in the price of gold. Gold can create parabolic trends with very fast price increases followed by sharp drops, which would be the ideal situation in which to have a protective put in place. The decline in gold prices in the early 1980s is a good example of what happens when a price spike is followed by an unexpected change in the underlying fundamentals and prices collapse. A lot of leveraged traders were wiped out when prices dropped that fast, and a protective put could have made the difference between severe losses and complete ruin.

In light of the fundamentals in the market, it seems unlikely that gold will collapse any time soon, but whenever you see gains such as those in the period 2003–2010, it is something to consider. Portfolio insurance is not free, and a protective put will be very expensive; however, there is also a great deal of flexibility in how expensive that insurance needs to be, and depending on your risk tolerance, you may be willing to get a little less protection in order to pay a lower premium.

Example of Buying a Protective Put

We will again assume that you are holding gold bullion ETF shares in your portfolio because they have very low fees, track gold prices very closely, and have extremely liquid options. Buying a protective put means you are purchasing enough long-term put option contracts to match the number of shares you are holding in your portfolio. If prices fall, the put will rise in value and offset some or most of those losses, depending on how far the market drops.

For example, on December 20, 2010, the SPDR Gold Shares ETF (GLD) was priced at $135.11 per share and a January 2012 put option with a strike price of $130 was selling for $8.10 per share, or $810 per contract. Traders who bought that put might not have been bearish but instead were looking for protection against a sudden and dramatic reversal in prices. If you held this put all the way until expiration and it remained out of the money, you would lose the entire investment. This is a bit like an insurance policy that you never needed to use. Depending on the trend in gold prices over the next 13 months, there are three basic scenarios that could play out.

Scenario 1: The Stock Rises, and the Put Expires Worthless

Assume that gold rose another 25 percent as it did in the previous 12 months and GLD is priced at $168.88 in January 2012. For a long-term investor this is a great outcome, but your returns will be lower than they would be if you held the unprotected position because you paid $8.10 per share to offset the potential for a major bearish reversal. You will have made a profit of 20 percent, but you took less risk.

Scenario 2: The Stock Falls, and the Option Gains in Value

Assume that instead of rising, GLD falls 25 percent to $101.33 per share by expiration in January 2012. Your put is now worth the difference between the stock price and the strike price ($28.67 per share), which can be added to the total value of your position. Unprotected long-term investors have lost 25 percent, but you have lost only 9 percent because the option has offset more than half of your losses. This result is good, but a protective put really pays off when the market is dramatically disrupted and prices fall very fast.

Scenario 3: The Stock Remains Flat, and the Option Loses Value

Perhaps GLD will remain perfectly flat and close in January 2012 at exactly $135.11 per share. Unprotected gold traders have lost nothing, but you have lost the option premium or 6 percent over that year. This would be a big disappointment, but depending on your overall risk tolerance, it may be an acceptable risk.

Protective puts are expensive but effective tools for capital preservation. Because of the expense, investors tend to be a little more selective about when to use them than they are with covered calls or naked puts. For example, few traders are interested in protective puts against gold when prices are moving slowly in a flat trend or during periods of economic uncertainty when gold prices are rising.

Practical Issues with Protective Puts

This is also not a very difficult strategy, but there are a few things to consider before you implement it in your portfolio.

Holding Shares in a Gold ETF and Selling a Protective Put at the Same Time Is the Same Thing as a Call Option

This sounds a little weird, but if you do the math, you will find that a protective put is the same thing as buying a long-term call option that represents the same number of shares. However, because long-term gold calls are more expensive than gold puts, you will wind up making less if the market rises, losing more if it remains flat, and losing slightly less if the market drops. This strategy is probably not a good trade-off.

You Do Not Need to Hold the Put All the Way through Expiration

Most long-term investors don't like to do much market timing, but selling the put when the risk factor you are most concerned about begins to fade is not a bad idea. Similarly, if you decide that you are going to rebalance your portfolio in the middle of the year and sell part of your gold holdings, you could reduce the number of put contracts by the same amount.

On a related note, if you don't feel that you need a full year's worth of protection, buying a protective put with a much shorter expiration will cost a lot less. For example, assume that you are concerned about the next Federal Reserve announcement, which is happening in a few weeks. You may decide at that point to buy a protective put with a short expiration before the meeting to insure yourself against a major disruption for a much smaller investment because you will need the protection for only a short time.

GOLD INVESTING THROUGH AN IRA

Gold can be held in an IRA (individual retirement account) as well as a standard brokerage account. For those without an IRA, there are basically two different types that vary with the time when you are taxed on the assets in the account. The first type of IRA, known as a traditional IRA, can be contributed to with pretax assets and is taxed later, when the assets are withdrawn. A Roth IRA works in the opposite manner in that you contribute after-tax assets that are not taxed when the money is withdrawn.

This explanation is a gross oversimplification but gives you the general idea. If you want to know more about what kind of IRA is right for you and when and how assets can be withdrawn for what kinds of taxes, you should talk to a qualified advisor. However, one way to look at it is that your choice of an IRA reflects what you think about future tax rates. An investor with a Roth IRA is betting that the IRA will be subject to tax rates that will be higher in the future, and so he is paying the tax now rather than later. A traditional IRA is just the opposite because you are charged taxes when you withdraw the money.

As a result of that difference we find that it is much more common to see investors elect to have a Roth IRA, because the general view that government taxes will rise in the future is a common opinion among gold traders. Regardless of when you pay your taxes, investors can actively trade gold and other assets within an IRA. You are not locked into your investments if you need to make a change. Despite the lower maximum contribution levels, this is just one of many reasons why an IRA is a better deal for savvy investors than a 401(k) plan.

Adding physical gold bullion to an IRA rather than gold stocks or ETFs is possible but can be a little tricky. First, you need to check with your IRA custodian to make sure it will allow that kind of investment, and you will need their help to roll over cash from your account to buy the gold with an IRS-approved dealer and storage company. This process can be complicated, and holding the gold will be expensive because you can't store it yourself. You also can't hold just any kind of bullion within an IRA; for example, several types of gold coins are not eligible.

It is very easy and cheap to hold a gold bullion ETF or gold stocks within an IRA, and most custodians wouldn't understand the difference between these "stocks" and anything else you hold in your brokerage account anyway. It is also possible to trade options within the brokerage account, but there may be some restrictions on what kinds of option strategies can be used. For example, some custodians will not allow option writing or spread strategies. You also need to keep in mind that if you are investing in gold companies, you may lose some of your tax-sheltered benefits on distributions if the firm is located outside the United States. In the gold market this is quite common as there is a large concentration of gold production companies in Canada, Australia, and South Africa.

Despite some of the drawbacks, investing in gold through a tax-sheltered account such as an IRA can be beneficial and is something you should investigate with your tax advisor and account custodian. Unfortunately, most 401(k) plans do not offer assets like this, and plan administrators aren't likely to add them as gold bullion ETFs do not charge high fees. Unless you happen to work for a gold company that offers an employee stock purchase program within your 401(k) plan, you may want to look into the options available to you through an IRA.

CHAPTER 8

Active Trading Strategies

The gold market is very active and liquid, which makes it ideal for short-term traders. For example, in 2010 gold futures set a new daily dollar-volume record of $55 billion in value, the SPDR Gold Shares ETF (GLD) trades an average $1.8 billion in value every day, and the London Bullion Market trades more than $24 billion in physical gold every month (at least that's the amount it discloses). To put this in perspective, all the North American stock and option exchanges trade an average of $8 billion per day in dollar volume combined.

All this volume means that the gold market is efficient, inexpensive, and flexible for short-term traders. The spread between the bid and ask prices on gold ETFs is often a penny or less, and options on the GLD often trade with a spread of a penny; that makes it possible to execute nearly any trading strategy you could imagine. We won't discuss every imaginable trading strategy in this section, but we have a few good ideas that you can use to get started as an active trader.

The concepts we will discuss next are riskier than those we used in the section about long-term investing because we will use leverage and market timing strategies to make profits from gold rather than using it to reduce account volatility. Leverage and short-term trades will always increase costs and risk compared with long-term investing, but for traders with a high risk tolerance and an interest in the gold market, there are very few markets that will be as productive as gold.

TRADING THE GOLD-TO-SILVER RATIO

Gold is imperfectly correlated with other precious metals, such as silver, which means that it trends differently. We will go into more detail about silver in a later section, but the reason they move differently has a lot to do with silver's greater sensitivity to the demand for hard commodities. However, these two markets are still close enough that a ratio between them will remain fairly flat for long periods. More than 100 years ago that ratio was 16, which meant that gold was 16 times more valuable per ounce than silver; however, as demand for the metals has changed, the ratio has shifted. Over the last few years the ratio between the prices of gold and silver has been channeling between 45 and 85 (at the extreme end of the range), which can be seen in Figure 8-1.

Traders use the gold-to-silver ratio to time trades between the two assets. The objective of this strategy is not to make profits but to increase the total volume of precious metals one owns. When gold prices are very high relative to silver, the ratio will be high and traders will sell gold to buy more silver. Eventually, when the ratio falls and silver's value compared with that of gold improves, traders will move back into gold. At the end of a successful swap you should own more gold than you would have otherwise.

For example, assume that in October 2008 you owned 1,000 shares of the SPDR Gold Shares ETF (GLD), which was worth $70 per share. At the same time, the iShares Silver Trust (SLV) was priced at nearly $8 per share. Because GLD's price represents one-tenth of an ounce of gold and SLV's price represents a full ounce of silver, you need to multiply by 10 to get the correct gold-to-silver

FIGURE 8-1

Gold-to-silver price ratio, April 2006–December 2010.

Source: iShares/SPDR Gold Shares

ratio, which at the time was 87 ounces of silver per ounce of gold. If you had known that this was an extreme move in the ratio and that it was likely to revert back toward its average in the next two years, you could have sold those GLD shares and purchased 8,750 shares of SLV with the proceeds.

Two years later, in October 2010, the gold-to-silver ratio had fallen to 56 and you could have reversed the transaction. At that point SLV shares were worth $24 and would have purchased 1,583 shares of GLD, which was priced at $132.62 per share. Because both markets went up, you would have made a profit, but your real accomplishment was to increase your holdings of GLD by almost 60 percent.

Short-Term Gold-to-Silver Ratio Trade Example

This strategy can be employed on a very short-term basis; for example, in January 2010 the gold-to-silver ratio spiked from 63 to

73, which created a good opportunity for active traders to swap GLD shares for SLV shares, anticipating that the ratio would return quickly to its short-term average in the low 60s. If you had 1,000 shares of GLD ($104.68 per share) on February 5, 2010, at the top of the spike, you could have purchased 7,285 shares of SLV for $14.37 per share. This trade has several potential outcomes, and like any trade, it can work against you if the ratio continues to widen while prices in both markets fall.

Scenario 1: Gold and Silver Both Rise in Price, and the Ratio Falls

By April 1, the ratio had returned to 63 and you could have swapped your shares of SLV for 1,159 shares of GLD. This is a 15 percent increase in your GLD holdings, and it has turned a potential 5 percent profit in GLD alone into a 22 percent gain over the same period. Making the trade on the basis of the gold-to-silver ratio increased your overall returns significantly because you matched the returns of SLV during that period.

Scenario 2: Gold and Silver Both Rise in Price, but the Ratio Continues to Climb

In this situation you are still profiting from a rise in SLV's price, but its purchasing power in gold is also falling; that means that you may decide to delay swapping your shares back for GLD until the ratio returns to its recent average. If the ratio never returns to the average, you will have made less than other traders who did not make a swap.

Scenario 3: Gold and Silver Fall in Price

In this scenario, you will lose more money if the ratio continues to rise than you would have if you had continued to hold GLD, but you will lose less if the ratio falls. For example, if you had made this trade from December 6, 2010, through January 7, 2011, your total losses would have been a mere 0.8 percent rather than the 4 percent GLD declined without the swap.

Other Factors to Consider

Market Timing Is Difficult

You are not concerned with whether the gold and silver markets go up when making trades based on the gold-to-silver ratio, but you are still making a trading decision that will succeed or fail on the basis of your ability to time the market. When using market timing strategies you will inevitably make some bad trades, so don't expect that you will come out in a better position after the swap. What you are planning for with this strategy is that over a large number of trades (or swaps) you will have done better than holding GLD itself over the long term.

This Is Designed for Investors with a Long-Term Bullish Outlook

This is a very popular strategy among traders who are willing to hold gold for the long term regardless of short-term ups and downs. Over the long term there is no guarantee that you will profit from the strategy, but we think that it is likely that your gold position will be less volatile overall.

Active Trading Increases Transaction Costs

Costs associated with this strategy come from commissions and fees as well as slippage, which can hurt your returns over time. Make sure that you are optimizing your expenses as much as you can. Depending on your broker and the frequency of your trades, it may even be possible to execute these swaps for free.

This is obviously a very simple strategy and is a unique twist on the concept of market timing; however, keep in mind that it is not designed to make profits but to increase your holdings in precious metals. Many traders feel that the gold-to-silver ratio is easy to predict because it tends to revert back to its short-term average, but those deviations can be quite extreme.

USING GOLD STOCKS AND GOLD TOGETHER

Gold and gold stocks are highly correlated, but their trends deviate from time to time, and those differences can be very useful regardless of which gold asset you are trading. The relationship between these two markets is similar to that between large-cap and small-cap stocks; like small-cap stocks, gold stocks are likely to rise faster than gold bullion during a bull market and lose more during a bear market or correction. That higher level of volatility can be a real benefit for gold traders who use the price action in gold stocks to time or trigger a trade in gold bullion ETFs or futures. In this way, gold stocks act as a nonlagging technical indicator to provide confirmation of a short-term buy or sell signal in gold prices themselves.

Because gold bullion is a larger market with more moderate fluctuations, longer-term signals such as reversals and divergences tend to be more reliable than they are for gold stocks. Gold stock investors should be very interested in the major reversal signals that appear in the bullion market because they are at greater risk if prices suddenly shift.

Example of an Intermarket Trade Signal

Figure 8-2 shows SPDR Gold Shares (GLD) on the left and the Market Vectors Gold Miners ETF (GDX) on the right. Both markets pulled back in October 2010, but bullion prices (represented by GLD) did not seem to be at an obvious support level. At the time, there was some evidence in favor of a bullish forecast in late October, based on a Fibonacci projection (see the technical analysis section of this book for more details), but confirmation of that sup-

FIGURE 8-2

SPDR Gold Shares (GLD) versus Market Vectors Gold Miners ETF (GDX), May 2010–November 2010

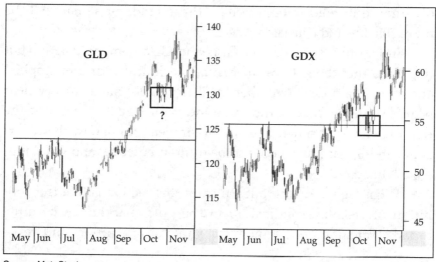

Source: MetaStock

port level would have been great. In the chart on the right, gold miners had pulled back to an obvious support level based on the multiple highs established that summer, which was just the confirmation that was needed.

Because gold stocks are more volatile than gold bullion, investor sentiment can be easier to identify and use in short-term trade timing. The signal we discussed could stand on its own for a trader willing to trade only GDX, but longer-term investors or traders looking for less volatility may prefer GLD and use GDX for signals. A second advantage of pairing the two markets like this and using GDX as a technical indicator is that it doesn't lag gold the way most technical indicators do.

What about Signals in Reverse?

This relationship between gold prices and gold miners also can be used in reverse. In the technical analysis section of the book we mentioned that bullish and bearish divergences are more clear and reliable when the market is quiet and the indicator lags prices a little. Gold stock investors may be very interested in a technical divergence in gold bullion, where these kinds of signals will be more reliable and consistent.

In Figure 8-3 you can see GLD and GDX compared again, but this time they both have an MACD technical indicator applied above the chart. On November 15, 2010, GLD signaled a very clear bearish divergence, but the same indicator on GDX signaled the risk of a reversal much later in December. Ultimately, the divergence in this case turned out to be quite predictive, and gold miners declined.

What we want you to learn from this section is that the definition of "technical indicator" in the gold market can be quite broad. Watching gold miners for short-term support and resis-

FIGURE 8-3

SPDR Gold Shares (GLD) versus Market Vectors Gold Miners ETF (GDX), September 2010–January 2011.

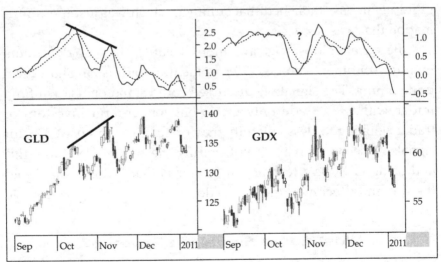

Source: MetaStock

tance levels is very productive for triggering trades in bullion itself, whereas the more moderate price action in bullion will produce major trend change signals that can be a benefit for gold stock traders because they are more reliable. This means that even if you trade only one type of gold asset, there are reasons to include other markets in your analysis. Additionally, besides reliable technical signals, including other gold markets in your analysis will increase your general awareness of the total gold market. That will help you make better long-term decisions in the long term.

Other Factors to Consider

There are a few tactical issues to deal with in adding an analysis like this to your trading.

Waiting for a Double Confirmation Won't Increase Your Success Rate

This can be a confusing issue for traders who assume that when there is agreement between more than one indicator or trading signal, the probability of a successful trade will go up. Waiting for signals from both the gold and gold mining markets to agree won't increase your probability of a successful trade. We discussed this issue (also known as indicator piling) more thoroughly in the technical analysis section of the book.

Adding Indicators Can Increase Trade Frequency Inappropriately

A related issue is the risk that adding more analysis will increase your trade frequency and costs in a way that will damage your account. Being a good analyst is often more a function of what you leave out than of what you include. This is good news because it gives you permission to limit your analysis to the factors you favor without feeling that you are missing out on something critical.

COMMITMENT OF TRADERS REPORT

In the futures markets there are three basic types of traders: large speculators such as the big banks and trading firms, small speculators or individuals, and large commercial hedgers. The aggregate positions of each trader type are broken out in a weekly report from the Commodity Futures Trading Commission (CFTC). It's called the Commitment of Traders (COT) report and is released to the public each Friday.

This weekly alert is a great analytical tool for traders because it provides up-to-date information about the strength of the trend in gold prices. If traders are overwhelmingly long or are increasing their long positions, there also will be a bullish bias in the market. Similarly, if traders are short or are increasing their short positions, we will be taking action to control our risk in long gold positions. However, not all traders are of equal importance; in fact, we may want to do the exact opposite of what some traders are doing in the gold market.

Commercial Hedgers

These traders represent companies and institutions (mostly gold producers and the bullion banks) that use the futures market to offset risk in the physical gold market. For example, a gold miner may short gold futures so that it can effectively "freeze" prices for future production. The gold miner is not bearish on gold but knows that if gold prices fall in the future, that could hurt its profitability. Selling a gold futures contract protects a trader's profits the same way a protective put option does. These traders are usually managing risk through futures, and so they typically do the opposite of what we do as speculators.

Large Speculators

This category (sometimes referred to as the noncommercials or "managed money") includes large institutional investors, hedge funds, and other entities that are trading gold futures for investment and growth. They typically are not involved directly in the production, distribution, or management of the underlying commodities or assets. We want to pay the most attention to this category because its interests are aligned with ours.

Nonreporting Traders

This is the catchall category for traders who are too small to be required to report their positions to the CFTC. We don't know how many individual traders there are or what kinds of investment strategies they are using because they are nonreporting. Most market professionals assume that a major percentage of these traders are individual speculators. As a group they are not going to be very accurate, and you will see them betting against the trend as often as they trade with it. You don't need to pay any attention to this category.

Knowing what the big speculators are doing through the COT report gives us some idea about the trend for gold because we can see what the so-called smart money is doing. It is difficult to get precise entry and exit signals from the COT report, and so its primary purpose is to help you identify and grade the strength of the trend. With the COT report acting as a trend indicator, you can use other analyses to time an entry in favor of a strong trend or choose when to apply greater risk control when the trend is weakening.

How the Report Works

The COT report is useful, but the raw data from the CFTC can be a little dense and confusing without some historical context. It is usually more helpful to see changes within the information over time rather than in the form of a single snapshot. Historical graphs of the COT report data can solve this problem very effectively.

You can find and examine the report by hand each week and construct a graph yourself by using Microsoft Excel. This will require some effort, but we recommend it because it keeps you close to the data, and since the report is updated only once a week, it doesn't require a lot of work. You can find the COT report and historical data on the home page of the CFTC's Web site at www.cftc.gov; however, if the thought of spreadsheets gives you chills, several free COT chart sources are available on the Internet. In Figure 8-4 we graphed the net long position of the large speculators from 2006 through 2010.

As you can see from Figure 8-4, the net long/short position of large speculators has been rising since the 2008 crisis, which is exactly what we would have expected to see. Looking forward over the next few years, we expect to see the same trend continue as more investors hedge and diversify against risks. As a trading tool the COT report also can be helpful in the short term by putting some additional definition behind the trend. When large speculators are reducing their net long positions, we should expect the trend to be fragile, and when they are increasing that positive posi-

FIGURE 8-4

Commitment of Traders report, net long managed-money positions, June 2006–December 2010

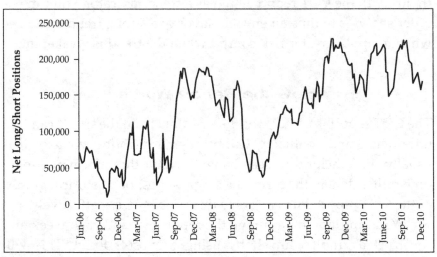

Source: CFTC

tion (especially after an unusual low), we should expect the trend to be very strong.

Commitment of Traders Report Trade Example

The last 18 months covered by Figure 8-4 consisted of three peaks in the net long positions held by large speculators. The most recent of those peaks began to break (bounce down from its own resistance level) in the middle of October, which was a signal for long traders to evaluate their positions and tighten up their risk control. From the middle of October through the end of 2010, gold's trend remained weak and additional risk coverage paid off.

The prior two peaks that established this chart's resistance level occurred in November 2009 and May 2010, both of which were followed by flat trends and declines in gold prices. Because the underlying fundamentals in the gold market are very bullish, we recommend against using these signals for contrarian trades. For example, following the bounce down in June 2010 with a short gold position would have been unwise now that we can see the subsequent rally through the third quarter; however, selling a covered call or even buying a protective put could have provided some protection against risk and some revenue during the soft trend.

Similarly, when the COT net long position is near a support level, as it was at the end of July 2010, we should feel a lot more confident about taking a little extra risk or entering new long positions. For example, buying long calls or an outright ETF position at these levels for a short-term opportunity would have been very profitable.

Other Factors to Consider

The COT report is a great source of information about gold trends and investor sentiment. Besides tracking large institutional traders, you can see what the major hedgers are doing and how heavily everyone is invested in the market. However, that transparency comes with a couple of key disadvantages.

The COT Report Lags

This report is very useful, but the data that are released on Friday cover only up to the previous Tuesday of the same week. Because the COT report is mostly a trending indicator, you shouldn't be too concerned about the lag, but once in a while something significant can happen before the report is released but after the Tuesday cut-off that makes the reading look a little strange.

The Smart Money Can Be Stupid

The large speculators or money managers are considered the smart money in the market, but they can still make bad forecasts. Using appropriate risk control and positioning will ensure you are not caught off guard when the smart money makes a big mistake.

TRADING WHERE YOU THINK GOLD WON'T GO

Put writing is a surprisingly controversial strategy but can be extremely productive for short-term gold traders as well as long-term investors. The controversy comes from confusion about whether it is more risky to write a naked put or to buy 100 shares of stock. As with most trading questions, the answer is somewhat nuanced. If the put is 100 percent cash-secured, the maximum risk is the same as it is with holding the stock. However, if you write a put and secure it with the minimum margin requirement (close to 20 percent of the underlying value), it is leveraged and will be more risky.

Selling a naked put is a bullish strategy because you want the put to become worthless, which will happen if the stock closes at expiration above the strike price. When you sell the naked put, you are paid the premium up front but will have to post margin to cover potential losses. You can make a rough estimate of how much margin will be required by multiplying the strike price by 20. You can also secure the put with the cash required to buy 100 shares of stock for the put's strike price. Depending on risk tolerance, most traders keep more margin than is required but stop short of securing the entire amount.

Comparison between Selling a Cash-Secured Put and a Long Stock Position

Imagine that you have a brokerage account with $13,800 available to buy 100 shares of the SPDR Gold Shares ETF (GLD) at $138 per share. There aren't any brokers out there who would prevent you from executing that trade because it has a fixed amount of risk that is covered completely by the stock.

Now imagine that you decide not to buy the stock and sell a naked put instead. Like the stock purchase, this is a bullish trade because you would like GLD to rise in value or at least stay above your strike price, which would make the put worthless, allowing you to keep the entire premium. Imagine that you sold an at-the-money put with 50 days to expiration, a strike price of $138, and a premium of $400. If the stock fell to zero, the put buyer definitely would want to exercise the contract and put the stock to you. This would result in the maximum (although unlikely) loss of $13,400 on the trade.

Wait a minute! The maximum risk of a short put is actually $400 less than buying the stock itself? Yes, it is, because the premium you received when you sold the put is yours to keep if the put is exercised or expires worthless. However, if you ask the average broker what the maximum risk is for a short put, he or she usually will respond "unlimited," which is the result of confusion between a short put and a short call option. A short, cash-secured put has almost exactly the same risk profile as a covered call, which is usually the first level of options approval for a retail account, whereas put writing requires the second highest level of approval.

Because put writing is an actively managed position, cost control is a big issue. For traders with a small account, costs can be very high relative to the amount of income generated. That may mean that this is a strategy to implement later, when your account is larger.

Example of Writing a Put

If you were confident that gold was going to rise in the short term, a call option, shares of an ETF, or a futures contract would be a better strategy than writing puts. Put writing is a good strategy when you are confident about where support is but aren't sure whether the market is going to move very far in the short term. A typical scenario for put writing occurs after gold has been in a very strong trend and has begun to consolidate a little. This situation allows you to trade where you think prices won't go rather than where they will.

For example, GLD rallied through November 2009 before pausing and beginning to channel over the next five months. This is a great opportunity for put writing because it's so common for gold to channel after a significant price move. You can see this setup in Figure 8-5, where gold hit the 104–108 support level six times in a row before finally renewing its trend in May. As long as the ETF stays above the strike price (the shaded area) through expiration, the put will expire worthless.

Selling a put with 35 days to expiration and a strike price of $100 (below support) would have paid a premium of $1.20, which would have resulted in a return on margin of 6 percent or a return of 1 percent on a cash-secured basis. That doesn't sound like much, but the annualized rate of return on a cash-secured put like this is almost 15 percent, whereas the annualized return on a margined trade is 100 percent. The small potential return from a single trade like this is offset by the high probability of a successful trade. GLD can rise in value, trend flat, or even decline a little without putting the trade at risk. The higher probability for a successful trade is one of the reasons so many investors use this strategy in the gold market.

FIGURE 8-5

SPDR Gold Shares, August 2009–May 2010

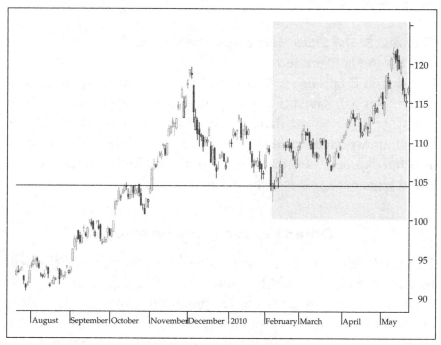

Source: MetaStock

When you are writing a put, there are three possible outcomes if you decide to hold the trade through expiration.

Scenario 1: The Stock Stays above the Strike Price by Expiration

In this situation, the put expires worthless and you keep the maximum gain. In the case of an out-of-the-money put, this is the most likely scenario each time you open a trade.

Scenario 2: The Stock Falls toward Breakeven below the Strike Price, and the Put Is Exercised

The trade will still make money as long as prices stay above $98.80, but the put could be exercised if prices are below the strike price.

As long as the difference between the current stock price and the strike price is less than the premium you were paid, the trade will be above breakeven.

Scenario 3: The Stock Falls below Breakeven, and the Put Is Exercised

Imagine GLD falls unexpectedly and closes at $90 per share at expiration. You will have the stock put to you at $100 per share, which would be an $8.80 per share loss on the trade. A move like this is clearly unexpected, but it happens once in a while. As a put seller you have to be aware that although a loss like this is unusual, it could wipe out a few months' profits.

Other Factors to Consider

Put sellers have to be very strict about their money management because a bad trade can be quite large. Keeping your positions small will help you resist the temptation to overtrade by exiting every time gold dips lower for a few days. Prepare yourself for some of the uncertainty of being a put seller by paper trading the strategy for several months before deploying it in your live account.

Larger Premiums Equal Bigger Risk

Many traders will sell puts with a strike price that is much closer to support to earn a larger premium. There is nothing wrong with that modification of the strategy, but a larger return will increase risk. The closer the put's strike price is to the stock price, the more likely it is that the put will expire in the money, which would result in a loss for you. This trade-off between larger profits and greater risk is normal in the financial markets.

You Can Buy the Put Back before Expiration

As in most trades, you are not locked into your trade and can buy the put back before expiration to take profits or stop-losses. In fact, many put sellers routinely exit their positions the Friday before expiration and then write the put for the next month. This can result in a slightly smaller return over time, but it decreases the risk of exercise.

Exercise Is Expensive

Having a put exercised is not a bad thing if you are not overleveraged, but brokers will charge larger commissions to handle exercise, and so avoiding it (if possible) is a good idea.

Turning the Put into a Credit Spread Can Limit Your Risk

If you bought another put with a lower strike price but the same expiration date, you can limit the risk in the trade to the difference between the two strike prices. That strategy is known as a vertical spread and makes sense in the right situation; however, it will reduce the potential return significantly. Usually, we don't recommend out-of-the-money credit spreads like this because they return a very small premium compared with the risk, but you may want to paper-trade them to see the performance.

INCREASING LEVERAGE WITH SYNTHETICS

Although we have discussed synthetic stock positions as a short-term strategy, there is no reason why they can't be used by long-term investors with a high risk tolerance. The primary difference would only be the time frame you are evaluating. After the strategy example we will go into more detail about other modifications you can make to accommodate a longer-term forecast.

A synthetic position is an options strategy that is designed to replicate the price movement of the underlying ETF shares with additional leverage. A synthetic position consists of a call and a put with the same expiration date, but one of the options is sold short while the other is held long. That means that one side is "naked" or uncovered, and you will need to post margin to make the trade. As we discussed in the last section, you can make a good estimate of the margin requirement for a particular trade by multiplying the strike price of the short option by 20, which means that 5:1 is the maximum leverage in this strategy. This is much larger than the maximum leverage you can access when purchasing or shorting stock (2:1) without integrating options.

A synthetic position can be created with a long call and a short put (synthetic long) or with a short call and a long put (synthetic short) to match your trade analysis. You have flexibility with expiration dates and even strike prices, but for this example we will keep it simple and use an at-the-money strike price and a short-term expiration.

Example of a Synthetic Long Position

In Figure 8-6 you can see that gold had recently hit all-time highs but was back to support on November 16, 2010, in the $130 range. Assume that you set a profit target equal to the prior high of $139.15 and set up your synthetic position with at the $130 money strike price and a December expiration. If a synthetic is established with a strike price very close to the current ETF share price, the credit from the short put should come very close to offsetting the price of the long calls. This can vary a little with what volatility and prices are doing at the time you enter the trade, but it is even possible for synthetics to be entered with a small credit if you time your entry right.

The trade is executed in two parts.

Leg 1. Buy to open the December 2010 calls at the 130 strike price for $3.05 per share, or $305 per contract.

Leg 2. Sell to open the December 2010 puts at the 130 strike price for $3.00 per share, or $300 per contract.

The trade will cost a debit of $5 per contract.

FIGURE 8-6

SPDR Gold Shares ETF, September 2010–December 2010

Source: MetaStock

As a percentage of the underlying value of the position, this is actually a relatively small investment; however, the total risk of this trade is not limited to the net debit of $5 per contract. If the stock drops on unexpected news to $100 per share, the call will be virtually worthless and the put contract will now be worth a minimum of $30 per share. Because you are the put seller, those losses are yours to cover. This seems an unlikely scenario, but it can happen and you shouldn't underestimate the risk of being in a long gold position when prices adjust very quickly. You will also need to post margin to hold the short put, and this is a more accurate estimate of how much you have *invested* in the trade. We can make a quick estimate of the margin requirement in this trade by multiplying the strike price of the short put by 20, which gives us a $2,600 margin requirement per contract.

Now that you know your margin requirement, our comment about using 5:1 leverage should make a little more sense. If you had purchased the stock outright, you would have paid $13,000 ($130 per share × 100 shares = $13,000). If you divide the underlying value of the position ($13,000) by the actual margin requirement ($2,600), the quotient will be 5—voilà! Using leverage will increase your purchasing power and potential profits, but you are taking five times the risk.

These positions are usually entered as a single order with both legs to be filled at the same time or neither of them should be filled. You can *leg into* the spread one side at a time, but you may wind up paying a higher bid-ask spread and more total commissions. It is also possible that you will need to have a talk with your broker before she will authorize your account to enter a short put position. Some brokers will approve you right away, and others won't.

How the Trade Compares with a Long Position

Imagine that you hold the trade until GLD has risen to the profit target of $139.15 per share. If you had held the stock itself, you would be up a tidy $9.15 per share, for a 7 percent return on investment. However, the synthetic should also be worth at least $9.15 per share, or $915 per contract. That is true because the put will now essentially be worthless (good for you as the seller) and the call has at least $9.15 in intrinsic value. However, because you invested only one-fifth of the cost of the underlying stock, you are now up 35 percent on the trade.

We stated earlier that if you have never traded gold options, you should practice this trade in a paper account several times before risking any money. The trade is high-risk, and position sizes should be kept relatively small compared with the rest of your portfolio.

Other Factors to Consider

There are a few more issues with trading a synthetic long position that you should consider before taking a trade like this.

Option Prices Don't Always Act as Expected

Option prices do not move in a perfectly linear way, and so it is possible that when you close the trade you will have made a little less or a little more than you expected. It is difficult to predict what will happen, but there may be a small variance in what you actually make compared with what you thought you would. This variance should be small and could be in your favor, but it more likely means you will be taking a small haircut on your profits.

Exercise Can Be Expensive

When you short an option, you are accepting the liability of early exercise. In this case, the put buyer could choose to exercise the option and put the stock to you for the strike price. Early exercise is relatively rare, but the further the put goes in the money, the more likely it becomes. You should discuss this risk with your broker so that if exercise happens and you wake up to see 100 shares of stock put to your account, you will know what to do about it.

You Can "Split" the Call and Put Strike Prices to Create a Modification

There is a popular alternative to the synthetic strategy called a combination, which is very similar to a synthetic but involves two different strike prices. Sometimes traders do this when gold prices are right in between two strike prices, and it can result in a net credit rather than a debit if the long leg is further out of the money than the short leg.

In the prior example assume that you had decided to buy the 131 calls for $2.65 per share and sell the 130 puts for $3.00 per share, which resulted in a net credit of $0.35 per share, or $35 per contract.

That credit should be enough to offset your commissions, but it will also result in slightly less upside potential.

Besides the credit there is another advantage of a combo over a synthetic position. If prices wind up going nowhere and GLD closes anywhere between the two strike prices, both options will expire worthless and you will get to keep the credit as a small profit. As you can imagine, this result is rare and probably shouldn't be the entire reason you opt for trading combinations over synthetics. Compare the two strategies while you are paper trading to get a better feel for how they compare and what market conditions might be best for each.

MONEY MANAGEMENT STRATEGIES

Position Sizing

Money management is one of the most neglected disciplines in trading, yet it can make the biggest difference in your overall profitability. Whenever we talk to a new trader who has blown up a large portion of his account (more common than you would think), the problem was almost always nonexistent money management. For an active trader this is more important than fundamentals, technical analysis, liquidity, or the account balance. Fortunately, it all comes down to two very simple concepts: Be consistent and trade small.

Being consistent is very simple because all it takes is making sure that your trades are of similar size. There are entire books about this subject (some are very good), but 90 percent of the benefits of the most elaborate position sizing strategies can be achieved by keeping your trade sizes consistent.

Trading small is imperative to being able to stay consistent. If you are trading very large amounts and have a string of losers (we all get them), you could wipe out a major chunk of your portfolio, which will make being consistent in your next trades very difficult.

Trading small can be difficult for traders with a small account in which even a single option or futures contract represents more than 5 percent of their capital. In these cases, we suggest staying with long-term strategies until you have contributed enough to your account to be able to use money management appropriately.

To implement a money management strategy in your short-term trading account you will need to determine what percentage of your portfolio you are willing to lose if a trade goes bad and how much per-unit risk is in a given trade—that's it. If you know the answers to those two questions, position sizing will be a snap because you will know exactly how much you should invest in any trade.

How Much Are You Willing to Lose?

This is much simpler to answer than you might think. Even though there are formulas that can give you the optimal percentage of your portfolio to put at risk in any single trade, it's usually better to start with a small figure and nudge it up or down over time as you get a feel for your own trading. We usually suggest starting with less than 5 percent but more than 1 percent of your total port-folio, but to make things simple we will use 3 percent as the amount we are willing to risk in our money management example.

This means that if you had a $100,000 portfolio and were will-ing to risk 3 percent in a specific trade, your trade size would be $3,000. Active investors usually deal with streaks of good and bad trades, but unfortunately, losses will not be evenly distributed among the winners. As you experience your own losing or winning streaks, your position size as measured in absolute dollars will rise and fall with your account balance, but the percentage you put at risk remains constant.

This part of the money management process is straightfor-ward and uncomplicated. It will be tempting to scale up in size when you have a streak of winners or to reduce the average trade size when you have had a bad run. Resist that urge and start out small enough that a few bad trades won't stress you out.

How Much Are You Willing to Risk per Trade?

This part of the process can be a little more nuanced when it comes to leveraged positions. For example, you could assume that when you buy a long call option, the risk of that trade is the entire premium, which is reasonable because option prices are volatile and can move down very quickly. However, it is probably not reasonable to assume that the risk of selling an option, trading a synthetic, or buying a futures contract is equal to the underlying value of those positions. For example, it may be possible for gold prices to fall to zero (resulting in the theoretical maximum loss for a short put, long synthetic, or long futures contract), but it is not practical for our purposes.

We usually recommend that if the leveraged position looks like a stock or futures contract, 20 percent of the underlying value is an adequate measure of risk. Therefore, if you are trading short options, the risk would be 20 times the strike price, or 20 percent of the underlying value of a futures contract. There are small improvements you could make to this strategy by accounting for volatility differences, but those changes fall within the remaining 10 percent of the possible improvements you can make with consistent position sizing. As you gather more experience, it will be easier to explore some of those subtle changes further without overwhelming your decision-making process.

How Big Is Each Trade?

Imagine that you are entering an at-the-money synthetic long position on GLD when it is priced at $150 per share. You have $3,000 at risk (the short put's strike price multiplied by 20) per contract, which means you can buy one unit in accordance with the maximum portfolio loss number we came up with earlier.

Here is another example that is slightly more complicated. Imagine you decide to buy a call option on NovaGold Resources (NG), which is a gold exploration stock that is priced at $13 per share. The 13 strike price calls with 60 days until expiration are trading for $1.40 per share, or $140 per contract. You know that you have $3,000 to risk in the trade, which means that you should buy 21 contracts to keep this position consistent with the other one you entered on GLD.

This is an easy calculation if we break it out one step at a time.

How much are you willing to lose? $100,000 portfolio balance $\times$ 3 percent maximum loss per trade = $3,000 maximum risk per trade

How much is at risk in the trade and how many contracts should you purchase? $3,000 maximum risk per trade/$140 price per contract = 21 contracts (rounded down)

Because active traders are doing so many things at once, if position sizing isn't simple, they don't do it consistently. Trying to make quick estimates can be difficult when the market is moving and you are feeling pressured; therefore, we recommend setting up a spreadsheet that tracks your portfolio balance and can be used to double-check your calculations quickly when you are entering a new trade. Working with a trading partner who can sign off on your trades before you make them is even better.

Trade Smaller to Make More Money

We mentioned the importance of trading smaller in the last section, but this concept merits more attention because it can seem a little counterintuitive to assume that trading small can improve your overall profitability. Trade size would not be an issue if winning and losing trades were evenly distributed, but they aren't, and you won't know how bad your worst streak will be until it happens.

Imagine that you start with an account of $100,000 and lose 20 percent on a very big trade, which means you now have $80,000 in your account. In the next trade you win 20 percent, but that does not get you back to breakeven because your account balance is now only \$96,000. You would have had to make 25 percent in the next trade to get back to breakeven. The problem of compounding losses gets worse very quickly when you have a bunch of losers in a row, especially if you are expecting to win or lose a large amount (in percentage terms) in each trade.

For example, in Table 8-1 you can see the breakdown of a trading competition among five different traders, all of whom are using different trade sizes. The competition started off with a streak of five losers and ends with a streak of five slightly larger winners. As you can see, the riskiest trader is still at a loss whereas the two smallest traders closed with profits.

Active traders tend to lose or win very large amounts compared with their per-trade investments, because they are often trading leveraged instruments such as options or futures. The big trader in Table 8-1 is at a disadvantage by the middle of the trading competition, because although she is willing to take more risk, she

TABLE 8-1

Trade Size Comparison Table

| Trade No. | Result | % of Portfolio at Risk | | | | |
		3%	5%	10%	15%	20%
		\$100,000	\$100,000	\$100,000	\$100,000	\$100,000
1	−100%	\$97,000	\$95,000	\$90,000	\$85,000	\$80,000
2	−80%	\$94,672	\$91,200	\$82,800	\$74,800	\$67,200
3	−75%	\$92,542	\$87,780	\$76,590	\$66,385	\$57,120
4	−100%	\$89,766	\$83,391	\$68,931	\$56,427	\$45,696
5	−20%	\$89,227	\$82,557	\$67,552	\$54,734	\$43,868
6	+75%	\$91,235	\$85,653	\$72,619	\$60,892	\$50,448
7	+100%	\$93,972	\$89,936	\$79,881	\$70,026	\$60,538
8	+80%	\$96,227	\$93,533	\$86,271	\$78,429	\$70,224
9	+100%	\$99,114	\$98,210	\$94,898	\$90,193	\$84,269
10	+50%	\$100,601	\$100,665	\$99,643	\$96,958	\$92,696
End Result		**+0.60%**	**+0.66%**	**−0.36%**	**−3.04%**	**−7.30%**

has a lot less capital to work with (after the string of losers) and her trade sizes will be very inconsistent.

The smallest investor has done reasonably well considering the losing streak at the beginning of the competition, and she has actually made a small profit. She is also able to be much more consistent from trade to trade because each winning or losing position has a smaller individual impact on the aggregate portfolio balance.

The table shows an overoptimized situation because the trades were all taken sequentially, which means that each trade was entered only after the last one had been closed and a new capital balance was known. This does not reflect reality very well because most traders are in many positions simultaneously. If the losing streak in the chart had happened when all five positions were still active at the same time, it would have wiped out the big trader completely.

If you are currently an active trader, you should put this concept to the test and find out whether you are using the wrong trade size. Export the trading history from your actual account and begin reducing the trade size in a spreadsheet, but keep the percentage gains and losses the same. If you have been consistent in your sizing, you should be able to tell easily whether you could have performed better with smaller trades. We have done this test with hundreds of traders, and the results are very revealing.

Although it is tempting to take big risks for theoretically bigger returns, trading too big over a series of many trades will reduce your returns in both percentage terms and absolute dollars even if you are winning more times than you are losing. Take the time to rethink how large your trades are and whether you are sacrificing performance.

Risk Control (Stop-Losses)

Pick up any book on trading and the subject of stop-loss orders will be featured prominently; however, this is a very delicate tool and can easily hurt you in the gold market when used inappropriately. There is no need to apply a stop-loss on all trades, and when it is used, a stop-loss order should only be expected to protect your portfolio from unexpected and catastrophic moves in the market. Unfortunately, many traders use very tight stop-loss orders as a way to delegate decision making to their computers; that is a misuse of stop-losses and will lead to higher costs and overtrading.

What Is a Stop-Loss Order?

Stop-losses or stop-market orders are conditional orders that go into effect once a trade has lost a predetermined amount of value. For example, if you bought shares in Barrick Gold Corporation (ABX) for $50 per share and set a stop-loss order at $45, your trade will be closed if the market drops to that level or lower without any need for you to be there physically to enter an order.

A stop-loss is actually a market order; that means that if prices reach the stop price, a market order will be entered to close the trade. A market order can be filled at a much lower price than expected. For example, if prices on ABX gapped from $50 to $40 per share overnight, your stop-loss will be executed, but it will be filled at $40 because that is the market price. Some brokers will allow you to set conditional limit orders that will be filled at your specified price or not at all, but those orders are not very popular as a way to control risk.

When to Use a Stop-Loss Order

Stop-losses are a good idea when you have a very large position in which a big unexpected move in price would be very damaging to your portfolio. Because the gold market is inherently volatile, stop-losses should be applied far enough from your entry price that you won't be "whipped out" on a small spike. Many traders are tempted to use very tight stop-losses because they are trying to avoid having to make a decision later, when it is time to close a losing position. Essentially, they are turning over a very important part of the trading process (closing a losing trade) to a computer, which will lead to being stopped out of a lot of trades, higher costs, and limited upside potential.

You should seriously consider whether you really need a stop-loss order when you are in a trade with fixed risk and high volatility. Long options are the perfect example of a situation in which a stop-loss order is more likely to hurt you than to protect your profits. Option prices are volatile and can be affected by price action, volatility, and time value erosion, all of which will contribute to large fluctuations in price. This rule is not absolute; there may be situations in which a stop-loss on a very long-term option, synthetic position, or spread is more reasonable.

We usually recommend that if you have a large number of trades being closed by stop-losses, they are probably too tight and you aren't taking responsibility for making your own exit decisions. If trading with a wide stop-loss makes you nervous, it is probably a signal that your trade size is too big, which can cause much more damage to your account than will a few runaway losses.

Stop-Losses Do Not Equal Risk

Traders often use a stop-loss as the "risk" in a trade when calculating position sizes. For example, a trader may assume that if he buys shares of ABX for $50 and then places a stop at $45, the maximum risk will be $5 per share, which will lead to a very large position size. That is a mistake because a stop-loss is a market order, and therefore your losses can be much larger than you anticipated. It is better to err on the side of a larger maximum risk number to keep your positions small and controlled.

Trailing Stop-Loss Orders Are Particularly Challenging

A trailing stop-loss is an order that is placed a specific distance below the most recent high prices in your trade. For example, assume that you bought ABX at $50 and at the same time set a $5 trailing stop-loss order, which would act like a normal stop-loss if the stock dropped directly to $45 after you had entered your position. However, if the stock moves to $60 right after you entered your order, the stop will "follow" that trade and now be at $55. That seems like a great strategy because the trailing stop-loss is protecting your profits as the trade grows. However, the problem with trailing stop-losses is that they tend to be executed on brief retracements within the trend. If the trailing stop-loss is following your trade very closely, it will lead to an early exit and reduced upside potential. In our experience, using a trailing stop-loss like this will lead to overtrading and a distorted risk/reward ratio.

A stop-loss can be an effective tool for risk control in the right situations, but it also can lead to problems that hurt your account. Make sure you are not using a stop-loss because your position size is too large or you are not adequately diversified. If you are being stopped out of trades frequently rather than making an intentional decision to exit, it may be time to reevaluate how you are using these tools and what changes you could make to your trade setups to prevent avoidable losses. An easy test you can use to see if this is an issue in your account is to export your trading history but modify all your stop-losses to be much wider. Would enough of the stopped trades have worked out profitably to make up for the larger losses in the others? Chances are good that you will find that your stops have been too tight and you have been missing out on potential profits.

CHAPTER 9

Gold's Sister Market: Silver

Silver and gold are similar in many ways but different enough to provide a little extra diversification within the precious metals market. You can invest in or actively trade silver with the same strategies you use in the gold market. As with gold, we recommend silver bullion ETFs, ETF options, silver mining stocks, and silver futures over bullion and spot dealers; however, silver is easy to invest in through physical bullion or coins if you choose to do that.

Silver is complementary to gold because although the markets shadow each other, they are not perfectly correlated and silver is more sensitive to economic growth. Many precious metals investors use this small difference to trade between the two assets. You may decide to hold gold when uncertainty and fear are at their highest but then move some assets into silver as fear begins to recede and growth improves. Figure 9-1 shows how the two assets have moved relative to each other since the financial crisis of 2008. Gold outperformed silver at the peak of the crisis but began to lose ground once recovery prospects began to improve.

The demand for silver has been so strong over the last two years that some traders are becoming concerned about a bubble.

FIGURE 9-1

Gold and silver bullion ETF prices, April 2006–December 2010

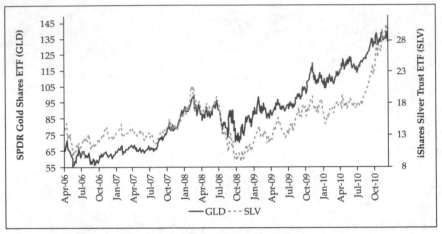

Source: iShares Silver Trust (SLV)/State Street Global Advisors (GLD)

The market is much smaller than the gold market and is therefore more sensitive to demand from speculators. For example, when the Hunt brothers failed to corner the silver market in 1980, the price of silver fell from $50 an ounce to less than $11 in two months. That led to an international panic, and Wall Street banks subsequently had to be bailed out (there is a long history of bailouts in the United States).

The Hunt brothers episode is an extreme example, but there are hints that we are seeing something similar if less coordinated today. Silver bullion money managers have been opening long futures contracts at an increasing rate, and the popularity of silver ETFs is also putting a lot of pressure on the market. All this excess demand has been good for prices, but it makes the market more fragile. These factors should contribute to additional volatility in the future, which is something to consider before you decide to make a long-term investment.

SILVER INVESTMENT PRODUCTS

Silver and gold investment products are very similar, with the same advantages and disadvantages; however, because silver tends to be more volatile than gold, you may prefer to use different strategies and products in the market. One difference between the two markets is liquidity, which means there are fewer viable choices for silver traders within each product class. For example, there is a very limited selection of silver mining stocks or silver mining ETFs that have a reasonable fee structure and adequate trading volume for most investors.

Bullion

The silver bullion market looks and acts almost exactly like the gold bullion market. If you plan to buy bullion, we recommend reputable dealers you can visit in person rather than mail-order companies that advertise in magazines and on the Internet. Silver bars and newly minted coins from reputable sources rather than "collectible" coins that carry a very large markup and are difficult to sell are usually the best way to buy the physical asset.

ETFs

Silver bullion ETFs are our recommendation for long-term investors to hold silver in the long term. They are less expensive than futures-backed or leveraged ETFs and will track the price of silver very closely. The same company (iShares) that offers the lowest-cost gold ETF (IAU) offers a silver bullion ETF (SLV) that has the largest market share in the industry. SLV is very liquid, with penny spreads and a very actively traded option chain. For almost all silver traders this will be the most efficient way to access the silver bullion market through a traditional brokerage account and/or within a tax-sheltered retirement account.

If you are interested in making a leveraged trade in silver, we highly recommend using options on bullion ETFs to avoid the issues of tracking error and higher costs that plague all leveraged and inverse ETFs. Although this requires a learning curve, the profits and flexibility available through silver ETF or silver futures options are worth the effort.

Silver Stocks

If you prefer the stocks of firms involved in silver mining and production, you will find that the pool of candidates is very thin. Many firms that mine, explore, and produce silver are also involved in gold production, so there is considerable overlap between indexes of gold and silver stocks. There are a few ETFs that cover the relatively small public silver production sector, including the Global X Silver Miners ETF (SIL) from Global Funds, but because the pool of stocks is relatively small, the fund is very concentrated and costs are high compared with other indexed ETFs.

Because so many stocks focused on silver production are located in emerging markets, they are also a good proxy for emerging markets equities. Having a global stock position in a well-diversified portfolio is a good idea, but be careful about buying both emerging market stocks and silver stocks as you may unintentionally be doubling up on the same kind of market exposure. Because of the significant overlap between companies involved in gold mining and silver mining, we recommend that unless there is a specific reason to have a concentrated exposure in silver stocks, a gold stock ETF probably will perform better.

Futures

Silver is a very actively traded product in the futures market. The largest and most actively traded contract represents 5,000 troy ounces, and like gold, it trades nearly 24 hours a day five days a week. There is a mini-version that is one-fifth the size of its big brother. Trading a silver futures contract is similar to trading a gold contract, with some very attractive benefits, including favorable tax treatment and leverage. Any trader willing and able to trade gold contracts would have no trouble integrating silver contracts into his portfolio.

FUNDAMENTALS OF THE SILVER MARKET

Silver is more sensitive to changes in industrial demand for commodities than gold is, but because it is also considered a store of value, it will benefit from demand for safe-haven investments. Change in the industrial demand for silver is one of the reasons it is much more volatile than gold, but it is also one of the reasons we expect silver to be more defensive than gold in a high-growth/high-interest-rate environment. There are several other fundamental factors that affect the silver market that we will discuss next.

Fear and Uncertainty

Silver is a compact store of value and is considered a safe-haven investment during times of uncertainty. In this way, silver acts a lot like gold; however, some investors prefer it in these market conditions because it costs less per ounce even though it tends to underperform gold.

Investment Demand

Silver is a much smaller market and is of less interest to the official sector (central banks) than gold; this means that large institutional traders can have a much greater impact on the market. For example, silver prices almost doubled in 1997–1998 because Warren Buffett's investment company acquired 130 million ounces. The market subsequently moved back to its historical trend, but

Buffett's purchase and the resulting short squeeze were a major factor in the unusual volatility.

In one respect this can be good news for traders who are bullish on silver in the short term. Although the big money can be unpredictable, the current trend is in favor of much more demand for silver as an investment over the next few years. For example, when the iShares Silver Trust ETF (SLV) was launched in 2006 it held 21 million ounces of the metal, but by the end of 2010 the ETF held almost 320 million ounces, which is nearly 50 percent of total annual production. You can see the amazing growth in SLV's assets in Figure 9-2.

It is very convenient and easy to invest in silver through an ETF, but just a few years ago that was not possible. It seems likely that demand for products such as SLV will continue to grow, which will put much more bullish pressure on the market in the short term. In the strategies section of the book we discussed an effective

F I G U R E   9-2

Growth of iShares Silver Trust assets (ounces), April 2006–December 2010

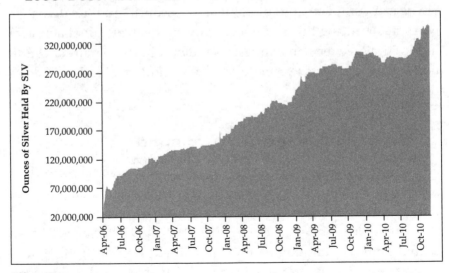

Source: iShares

gold/silver trading strategy that you can use to acquire shares of both SLV and the SPDR Gold Shares ETF (GLD).

Industrial Demand

Most annual demand for silver is for industrial applications, photography, and jewelry. Silver is the best known electrical conductor, so we expect that demand for silver in new technology will continue to rise as technology is integrated into more aspects of our professional and personal lives. This also means that silver will be more sensitive to changes in growth and inflation expectations than is gold. Commodities tend to rise in price when economic growth and inflation are anticipated in the near term, which could make silver a more effective inflation hedge than gold.

Silver bridges the gap between precious metals as a store of value and precious metals as a commodity, and for that reason there are many traders who prefer it to gold. We agree that silver is an attractive asset class and in certain circumstances might outperform gold; however, it is not different enough to be its own asset class on an equal standing with gold in a well-diversified portfolio. If you are inclined to use silver in your investing, we recommend splitting your precious metals allocation between silver and gold rather than adding more exposure to the same market.

CONCLUSION

Gold is playing a new role in the global financial markets. More investors have access to it than ever before, and the barriers to entry are likely to continue falling over the next few years. Although it has been a great source of profits over the last 10 years, it will continue performing best as a hedge against uncertainty and volatility in one's portfolio. We believe that the disruptions in the financial markets that were seeded in 2001 and began to blow in 2008 have just begun and that gold will be not only a source of profits but the best source of stability in the future. Therefore, we expect investors to continue using gold as the world's premier safe-haven investment for the next several years.

The goal of our book was to help you understand the opportunities in today's gold market as well as some of the greatest risks. We wanted to make sure that the book was practical, and so we prioritized discussions on the basis of products and strategies rather than politics and speculation. We hope that has been useful for you as a portfolio manager. We expect that there are many more changes and innovations in store for gold investors in the near future, and we are excited to be part of it.

As you begin working in the gold market, remember to do your own research. Much about forecasting and investing in gold is subjective and depends on one's point of view and investing objectives. We hope that as you become more involved, you will find yourself disagreeing with some of the recommendations we made because you will have found investment alternatives that are optimal for your account and capital balance.

We also want to provide a list of great resources to continue learning about the gold market. This list is not comprehensive, but it does represent what we feel are the best resources available to stay up to date on current events that affect the fundamentals of the market and gold investment products. Best of all, most of these resources are available for little or no cost. Use the money you save to buy an extra ounce; we think you will be glad you did.

ADDITIONAL RESOURCES

TOOLS AND EDUCATION

Learning Markets: www.LearningMarkets.com. This is
our site where we offer free daily videos and commentary
about trading strategies in the gold, stock, and forex
markets.

Chicago Board Options Exchange: www.CBOE.com. This
site is an excellent resource for daily market commentary,
videos, and education from the largest options exchange
in the country.

Options Industry Council: www.888options.com. Funded
by options brokers, this site has excellent tutorials that
range from the most basic introductions to very advanced
strategy analysis.

FINVIZ: www.finviz.com. The best source for free charts
of stocks and futures, this site includes a great search tool
for finding gold and silver stocks.

World Gold Council: www.gold.org.   The World Gold Council offers a great source for research and statistics at this site.

Gold Anti-Trust Action Committee: www.gata.org.   If the World Gold Council represents the "establishment" in the gold market, GATA represents the insurgency.

Freestockcharts.com.   Excellent interactive charts that include Fibonacci analysis can be found at this site.

NEWS AND ANALYSIS

Index Universe: www.indexuniverse.com.   Index Universe provides great commentary on money flows, ETFs, and portfolio strategies at this site.

CME Group: www.cmegroup.com/trading/metals.   The CME is the largest North American futures exchange and has some great educational material and analysis on its Web site.

Kitco: www.kitco.com.   Kitco's site includes spot prices, historical data, news focused on the metals markets, and great videos.

Hard Assets Investor: www.hardassetsinvestor.com. Hard Assets Investor is a commodities blog that you will disagree with as often as you will agree but will always enjoy.

Forex Factory: www.forexfactory.com.   Forex Factory is the best online source for economic calendars and analysis.

INDEX

ABOUT THE AUTHORS

John Jagerson and **S. Wade Hansen** are the founders of Learning Markets, which helps individual investors take control of their investment portfolios. They are also the authors of *All About Forex Trading* and *Profiting with Forex*. Jagerson and Hansen live in the Salt Lake City, Utah, area.